THE LONDON WELLNESS GUIDE

Edited by
Jeffrey Young

Author Allegra Strategies
Project Manager Becky Hindley
Content Writer + Researcher Marina Martyn-Hemphill
Reviewers Eilidh Hargreaves & Lara Murphy
Intern Erica Jungkurth
Photography Dan Carter & provided by venues
Design John Osborne
Website Tim Spring
Publisher Allegra Publications Ltd

D1395671

Visit our website:

www.londonwellnessguide.com

London Wellness Guide

All information was accurate at time of going to press.

Published by *Allegra* PUBLICATIONS Ltd © 2017

Walkden House, 10 Melton Street, London, NW1 2EB

FOREWORD

SIMON HILL-NORTON, SWEATY BETTY

In a strobe-lit room, a large group is moving in tune to a thumping beat. Down a chandelier-lit corridor, a brightly-dressed crowd lounge on sofas, sipping jewel-coloured drinks. This could be your typical nightclub, apart from the drinks are juice-based, the 'dancefloor' is strewn with weights and Pilates rings, and it's 7am. It's wellness, but not as you know it.

Step back to 1998, when my wife Tamara and I founded Sweaty Betty in Notting Hill. Despite being a healthy, fit area with a Pilates studio nearby our shop, the majority of London was a sparse space of chain gyms and the occasional vegetarian juice bar. Despite women working out and taking an interest in healthy living, it's safe to say the wellness scene wasn't anything like it is today. Then in stepped New York and Los Angeles. In Manhattan, New Yorker's take working out very seriously, and this combined with a Californian attitude to wellbeing, has transformed the way we think, move and shop.

Now going to the gym is a well-rounded experience, with body composition checks, personal training, smaller class sizes, luxury toiletries and on-site smoothies. Boutique fitness has transformed the wellness space, making working out and staying well a priority. In the last three years, new studios have opened throughout the city which celebrate fitness as fun. It's great to see this in London, Soul Cycle is huge in the states and I remember attending my first class and being blown away. There is a similar vibe at new indoor cycling, Pilates, HIIT and barre spaces here, which is undoubtedly why they have become so popular. This was enhanced by the introduction of Classpass in 2014, as it offered customers the chance to try out the best classes in the capital, minus the commitment.

This lifestyle shift has gone far beyond the studio though. London is now brimming with cold-pressed juice bars, healthy eating spots, mindfulness centres, spas and of course, shops selling beautiful activewear. When we founded Sweaty Betty it was with an aim to create clothing that transcends fitness. At this time women's sports gear was hidden away in the back of the local sport shop, whereas now stylish trend-led activewear is front and centre. Now with the wellness industry booming, leggings are officially the new denim with more and more women looking for clothes they can wear straight from a class to drinks with friends.

Social media has played a big role. Ten years ago we were limited to the offerings of the local gym, cookbooks or by what our friends were into - now the internet has opened up a global community to engage with. There's a tour de force of women including Ella Mills (aka Deliciously Ella), Amelia Freer and Madeleine Shaw posting about where they eat, workout and try the latest reflexology treatment. Instagram feeds have become the new little black book.

This transformation has lead me to the conclusion that 'wellness is the new rock and roll'. We're swapping the pub for indoor cycling classes, cocktails for green juices and clubbing for meditation. Wellness has become part of our general mindset, there is no one-size-fits-all approach, which is why it's fantastic to see the sheer range on offer in London. What's next? I predict fusion fitness, the importance of breathing and the introduction of more US studios in the UK. One thing I can guarantee: our support office team will still be on PSYCLE's website every Monday at 12, urgently refreshing to get a bike in their favourite class.

CONTENTS

INTRODUCTION

Welcome to the first edition of The London Wellness Guide - your ultimate guide to food, fitness, mind, body and soul.

Our mission has been to compile and review the fantastic assortment of places around London shaping modern perceptions of wellness and personal wellbeing. We have energetically scoured the city to bring you the best venues, activities and spaces for a healthier, more proactive lifestyle. This guidebook meanders from meals to meditation, high-intensity interval training to health food stores. Specially designed to keep you on your toes, the chapters purposefully hop from juice bars to ballet bars and handle bars, in an attempt to share with you London's multi-dimensional world of wellness.

When it comes to healthy eating, it's great to see cafés, delis, restaurants and juice bars embracing a new approach to their menu, one that's fresh and natural. Fast food is no longer synonymous with processed food, the game is changing and we're all learning that we are a product of what we eat - so we need to eat well. The places featured in this guide have been chosen not only for their healthy, feel-good food, but also for their ethos and atmosphere, their ethical values and friendly customer engagement.

And for those looking to get in shape, whether you're searching for classes in ballet, boxing, or an interesting fusion of the two, we've left no gym tyre unturned in our quest to find the right training space

to put your stamina to the test. The fitness section inside this book demonstrates how diverse the sector is and how fun and innovative workouts are becoming. We also aim to help you in your quest to find that luxurious health club, calming yoga session or snazzy dance studio that's right for you.

Just as there is plenty to get your heart pumping, there is also plenty to slow you down and give you a much-needed time out. London offers a world of opportunity, inspiration and excitement, but at times it can also feel crowded and seemingly out of your control. The spas, wellbeing centres and meditation spaces in the Mind, Body, Soul section show you where you are able to find serenity and calm within the hustle and bustle of this big city.

This book also includes a curated range of fascinating articles authored by industry experts, covering topics such as: gut health, the journey of yoga, starting a blog and the importance of sleep. We would like to extend a particular thank you to all of our contributors for their knowledgeable and insightful articles. Not simply a guidebook, this is a manual and a point of reference for those looking to make positive changes to their London lifestyle.

Enjoy the journey of discovery upon which you are about to embark!

FOOD

CAFÉS, DELIS + FOOD TO GO

VEGAN + VEGETARIAN

HEALTHY RESTAURANTS

JUICE BARS

HEALTH FOOD STORES

HEALTHY HIGH STREET

ONLINE DELIVERIES +
SUBSCRIPTIONS

FARMERS' MARKETS

OPEN

MON-FRI.	8:00AM - 9:30PM
SAT.	9:00AM - 9:30PM
SUN.	10:00AM - 4:00PM

🌐 26GRAINS.COM

⊖ COVENT GARDEN

26 GRAINS

1 NEAL'S YARD, COVENT GARDEN, WC2H 9DP

26 Grains offers a healthy dose of hygge with every hot bowl of banana cacao porridge. For those that haven't heard of 'hygge' (the wellness word of the moment) - this is a Danish concept used to express that cosy, warm feeling you get when you're nicely snuggled up and feeling content. Founded by Alex Hely-Hutchinson following a year spent in Copenhagen, this charming little place is located on the corner of Neal's Yard in Covent Garden. On entry you'll be greeted by a particularly distinctive smell; one that brings to mind dressing gowns, newspapers and soft slippers worn on a Sunday morning. Pots and pans hang above the stove and friendly servers wait to take your order before you take your seat. The menu is a glorious combination of innovative, nutritious and delicious recipes. Capitalising on nostalgic recollections of porridge, different types of grains are used as a base for nearly every option. The savoury Hygge Bowl or the sweet Nordic Pear porridge would certainly keep Goldilocks happy here.

BEL-AIR

54 PAUL STREET, SHOREDITCH, EC2A 4LN

OPEN

MON-FRI.   7:30AM - 5:00PM

SAT-SUN.   CLOSED

🌐 BEL-AIR.CO

⊖ OLD STREET

You can't miss the yellow and white striped awning on Paul Street, complete with a large black cartoon outline of a pineapple. Welcome to Bel-Air. Named after the famous Los Angeles neighbourhood, this venue exudes rays of Californian sunshine, despite its East London location. The café is super simple, light and refreshing, with a couple of tables for those who wish to eat in. 'Keepin' it real' is the slogan stamped on the wall, and so it seems. With an entirely freshly cooked menu of salads and lunches inspired by different countries - try Ethiopian beef wat braise, or coconut and pumpkin daal - Bel-Air is about seasonal, nutritious food that's made with passion (no microwaves here). Peek into the open kitchen to catch a glimpse of the chefs in action. They claim to use only the best fruit and vegetables, sustainably sourced and reared fish and meat, and no refined sugar. Post-workout, try the appealingly named Muscle Beach, steak served on a sweet potato and spinach hash with a poached egg on top. Finish your meal with an espresso because, really, what is an East End café without top notch coffee? Here, they serve Ozone; roasted only a few minutes away. One for the road?

THE BODYISM CAFÉ

224 WESTBOURNE GROVE, NOTTING HILL, W11 2RH

OPEN

MON-SAT. 7:00AM - 6:00PM

SUN. 8:00AM - 6:00PM

 BODYISM.COM

NOTTING HILL GATE

The Bodyism Café takes guilt-free indulgence to a whole new level with their cinnamon and honey cake. We couldn't help but float in to this healthy haven given that the food on offer is created with organic, unprocessed ingredients in mind as opposed to a restrictive calorie count. This means that there's no shortage of naturally sweet treats for the sweet toothed among us. Whether you're tempted by the Berry Burn shake, Charlotte's Strawberry Jam Toastie (using sugar-free berry compote), or the array of

acai bowls - there is certainly something to nibble on without being naughty. Though we should say, the Bodyism signature coffee, blended with grass-fed organic butter and virgin coconut oil, is not for the faint-hearted.

THE CANVAS CAFÉ

42 HANBURY STREET, SPITALFIELDS, E1 5JL

OPEN

MON. CLOSED

TUE-FRI. 9:00AM - 9:00PM

SAT. 10:00AM - 8:00PM

SUN. 10:00AM - 6:00PM

THECANVASCAFE.ORG

LIVERPOOL STREET / SHOREDITCH HIGH STREET

It's the writing on the walls that exemplifies this not-for-profit café's mindful, positive spirit. Bold black lettering asks things like, "Where are you from?", "What's the best thing that's happened today?" "Tell us about your grandparents." Thousands of replies in grey marker pen scrawl the walls, more appearing every hour. The Canvas Café is London's first ever 'happy café' and plays host to the Museum of Happiness, located in an outhouse accessible via the garden. True to Shoreditch form, Square Mile specialty coffee is served, along with a lunch menu that varies daily, and a

simple-but-tempting brunch list with vegetarian and gluten free options. Sure, this café is no-frills, but it's homemade charm, mindful ethos and delicious menu make it the perfect place to stop by, take a breather and smile.

CORE-COLLECTIVE.CO.UK

 HIGH STREET KENSINGTON

CORE KITCHEN

45 PHILLIMORE WALK, KENSINGTON, W8 7RZ

Attached to Core Collective - a super snazzy boutique fitness studio just off the High Street Kensington - Core Kitchen is, in its own right, a top recommendation for breakfast, brunch or lunch. The Australian-inspired menu makes sure your pre and post-workout energy levels are never below ready. Clearly high-intensity training deserves high-intensity taste. There are no words for their creamy coconut porridge topped with bananas and homemade granola, though the Green Bowl: kale, spinach, chard, avocado, poached eggs and dukkah, is also a core favourite. The problem here is whether to opt for the spirulina smoothie bowl or the dairy and gluten-free buckwheat waffles with coconut cream, blueberries, cinnamon and salted coconut caramel? The staff will tell you the solution to this is simple - get both. The discreet location of this kitchen draws in a particularly fast set, wearing the latest in athleisure looks it makes for prime people watching. With spread out seating and a large sofa to one side, the Instagram friendly-décor means you won't be able to resist uploading that photo of your lovely looking food. #COREblimey

DAISY GREEN

20 SEYMOUR STREET, MARYLEBONE, W1H 7HX

OPEN

MON-FRI.	7:00AM - 6:00PM
SAT.	8:00AM - 6:00PM
SUN.	9:00AM - 6:00PM

🌐 DAISYGREENFOOD.COM

⊖ BOND STREET

Founded by ex-investment banker Prue Freeman, Daisy Green offers a fanciful escape from the grey concrete of London's streets. Duck heads below deck and head downstairs in this Grade II listed building to find an Alice in Wonderland-esque seating area. Kitted out with kooky flowers hanging from the ceiling and colourful artwork by British street artist Shuby painted on the walls, the secret garden vibe resonates well with the fresh, Australian-inspired food. The weekly salads are all vegetarian and protein options include chicken skewers, turkey balls and falafel should you be looking to grab n' go. The option of organic cold-fermented activated charcoal sourdough with avocado, labne, lime & lemon is one to look out for. For those health heroes out there, the Vegan Nut smoothie (made up of banana, cashews, vanilla, Maldon sea salt, chia seeds, almond milk & agave) is sure to super fuel your fire! But be warned, you'll leave this place with more energy than the Mad Hatter...

OPEN

MON–SUN.   8:00AM – 9:30PM

 DAYLESFORD.COM

 SLOANE SQUARE

DAYLESFORD CAFÉ

44B PIMLICO ROAD, CHELSEA, SW1W 8LP

There's a countrified charm to the Daylesford Café that is otherwise very difficult to find in the centre of London. Selling only organic, seasonal food, this Pimlico farmshop and café is a hive of fresh produce and feel-good charm. Based on the Gloucestershire roots from which it's come, this dual-level deli and all-day café is designed in the style of a converted country barn. Sourcing the majority of its food from their Daylesford farms in the Cotswolds and Staffordshire, you can see and taste the difference in their natural and passionate approach. The brand ethos encapsulates wellness in its most wholesome form, where focus lies on sustainable farming, avoiding artificial growth promoters and animal hormone injections. The menu combines produce from the farm's market garden, its bakery, creamery and butcher. The upstairs area with a few long tables mixed with smaller tables makes this a great choice for any time of day.

THE DETOX KITCHEN

10 MORTIMER STREET, FITZROVIA, W1T 3JJ

OPEN

MON-FRI.   8:00AM - 7:00PM

SAT.   9:00AM - 5:00PM

SUN.   10:00AM - 4:00PM

🌐 DETOXKITCHEN.CO.UK

⊖ OXFORD CIRCUS /
   GOODGE STREET

Lily Simpson, one of London's wellness entrepreneurs, set up The Detox Kitchen with the desire to make clean eating more wholesome and delicious. The creamy courgetti dish certainly reflects this approach to healthy food. With the seasonal, bright bowls of good-looking salads and mains, it's hard to know where to start and when to finish. The bright spacious seating area has a mixture of small and large tables, highly recommended for group hangouts as well as one-on-one meetings. Situated in the heart of central London, just off Oxford Street, the white tiled walls and turquoise colour scheme infuse a sense of tranquillity over the everyday noise. Little added extras like the mint and lemon in the water jugs on the tables make the overall eating experience that much more pleasurable. Though it's called The Detox Kitchen, there's no shortage of sweetness here, free-from cakes and muffins are placed in a tempting spot next to the pay point. Head downstairs to find Studio 1 by The Detox Kitchen - a fitness space that runs a weekly schedule of energising classes. Make sure to pre-order your post-workout smoothies before the session starts!

FARMER J'S

107 LEADENHALL STREET, THE CITY, EC3A 4AA

OPEN

MON-THU.	7:30AM - 9:00PM
FRI.	7:30AM - 3:30PM
SAT-SUN.	CLOSED

 FARMERJ.COM

 ALDGATE

This East-End eatery is about good, honest food and humour. "We're cooks, not heater-uppers," they joke. But seriously, with 90% of produce freshly prepared on-site every day, seasonally-sourced ingredients from quality high-welfare farms, and a price list that's light on the wallet, it's a brilliant venue to relax and fuel up. The eatery is known for its Field Trays, "a main and a grain, with two sides and a sauce on us." Where else in London can you buy 24-hour marinated flank steak, flash grilled as you watch, with two sides and some

rice for £7.50? The seating area upstairs contains bar-style window seats and a huge sharing table, amongst a series of smaller ones; ideal for escaping the office, or simply discovering authentic, healthy food that packs a flavoursome punch.

GOOD AND PROPER TEA

96 LEATHER LANE, FARRINGDON, EC1N 7TX

OPEN

MON-THU.	8:00AM - 6:00PM
FRI.	8:00AM - 5:00PM
SAT-SUN.	CLOSED

 GOODANDPROPERTEA.COM

FARRINGDON

What began as a mobile brew bar in a 1974 Citroën-H van has become one of London's trendiest tea shops. Serving black tea, green tea, oolong tea, white tea, herbal tea and workshop coffee, they are bringing back what the British do best. The delicious 'Teatox' menu includes their healthiest options: matcha to focus the mind, turmeric to increase antioxidants, cacao to lift your mood, lemongrass and ginger to aid digestion and rooibos to improve circulation. The Crumpets are a little bit naughty but oh-so necessary to the overall experience! The shop

itself is artistically fresh and creatively cool. With exposed brick, chalk boards, bleached pinewood tables, framed photos of the van on its earliest escapades and glass containers filled with tea and hanging lamps, Good & Proper is East London trend-tea.

THE GOOD LIFE EATERY

59 SLOANE AVENUE, CHELSEA, SW3 3DH

OPEN

MON-FRI.   7:30AM - 8:00PM
SAT.   8:00AM - 7:00PM
SUN.   9:00AM - 6:00PM

 GOODLIFEEATERY.COM

 SLOANE SQUARE

   WC

The brainchild of Yasmine Larizadeh and Shirin Kouros, The Good Life Eatery is where street style gets freshly seasoned. The no Wi-Fi policy is in line with their purist attitude toward food: keep it original, keep it fresh and keep it inclusive. With a menu that's hearty, filling and indulgent yet healthy, the ethos here makes nutritious food feel cool, not clinical or confusing. This edgy hangout uses food (and delicious juice) to bring people together, you'll see people reaching over to try each other's egg white frittata or zucchini fettuccine. The Good Life prioritise locally sourced produce as they see it to be the greenest way of getting your 5-a-day. And they don't just buy local but they promise to serve local, consciously employing people from their own and neighbouring areas. With a no-reservation policy, the wooden tables (made from reclaimed furniture) can be hard to get hold of! But if you manage to make it here for breakfast, lunch or dinner, you'll realise how good life can be...

THE GOOD YARD

UNIT 19, THE ARCADE, LIVERPOOL STREET, ECM 7PN

OPEN

MON-FRI.   7:30AM - 4:30PM

SAT-SUN.   CLOSED

🌐 THEGOODYARD.COM

🚇 LIVERPOOL STREET

Find sanctuary on ever-bustling Liverpool Street at The Good Yard; a wholesome healthy eatery and espresso bar, tucked away in The Arcade. Expect a small, personable, no-fuss venue that serves up delicious, well-balanced salads, breakfasts, snacks, shakes and juices. Accessible price points and friendly, engaging service ensure city workers return daily to refuel at mealtimes and often in-between for the highly revered Square Mile coffee. Popular menu mainstays are their signature hot salads (smoky chipotle chicken, chorizo or halloumi), which will leave you zinging with energy, rather than hankering for sorely-missed calories. If you're after a quick fix, aptly-named juices, like Immune and Flu Fix, are freshly blended before your eyes and will certainly boost you through the day. Wooden tables outside the café in the arcade and an array of independent magazines at your disposal make for a peaceful setting, which is particularly refreshing on a glorious summer's day. Don't leave without picking up 'vegan, gluten-free, sugar-free amazeballs' (energy balls, to us). Made by Celeste Wong, a.k.a. well-known coffee blogger The Girl in the Café, they are famous amongst regulars.

THE HIVE OF VYNER STREET

286 - 290 CAMBRIDGE HEATH ROAD, CAMBRIDGE HEATH, E2 9DA

OPEN

MON-FRI.	8:00AM - 10:00PM
SAT.	9:00AM - 10:00PM
SUN.	10:00AM - 10:00PM

 THEHIVEWELLBEING.COM

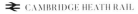 CAMBRIDGE HEATH RAIL

The Hive of Vyner Street has floor to ceiling glass windows. This means you get your daily dose of Vitamin D at the same time as you sip your cold-pressed Vitamin C (carrot, orange, red pepper and lemon). Both an organic café and a natural wine bar, The Hive has an open-plan layout with long wooden benches that make it a great place to co-work, co-eat and co-enjoy a Matcha latte. Serving breakfast, lunch and dinner, the East London workshop vibe transforms into a relaxed date space come sunset. We're told the cashew and pistachio brownie

is a winner whatever the time of day. With an abundance of vegetarian, vegan, and gluten-free options, the menu experiments with seasonal food and flavours and even their wine is organic and biodynamic. Bottle for two?

LU-MA CAFÉ

43 WORPLE ROAD, WIMBLEDON, SW19 4JZ

OPEN

MON-FRI.	7:00AM - 4:30PM
SAT-SUN.	8:00AM - 4:30PM

 LU-MA.CO.UK

 WIMBLEDON

Think of Wimbledon and it's likely that tennis championships, Pimms and strawberries and cream spring to mind, but Lu-Ma puts this South London spot on the map for another reason. Opened in 2013, this independent café serves a hearty dose of guilt-free goodness to those in the know. Breakfast is served from 7am and lunch from midday, and everything is dairy and refined sugar-free. They don't serve red meat but instead the dishes are centred around fruits, vegetables, legumes and grains. With large chalk boards, exposed brick walls and sanded

pine tables, the décor matches the Turmeric latte - warm and alluring. In the open fridge you'll find Blend & Press cold-pressed juice, a selection of raw Lu-Ma desserts (all vegan, sugar-free and gluten-free) as well as coconut water, kombucha and Rebel Kitchen mylk.

THE MAE DELI

18 - 20 WEIGHHOUSE STREET, MAYFAIR, W1H 5BH

OPEN

MON-FRI.   7:30AM - 9:00PM

SAT-SUN.   9:00AM - 9:00PM

 THEMAEDELI.COM

 BOND STREET

Its very own ray of sunshine, Deliciously Ella's latest venture, The MaE Deli, notably brightens up the block. Situated on the corner of Weighhouse Street, the interior of this red-bricked deli looks as fresh and clean as the food it serves. The design is sleek and well thought out, with large windows letting in the natural light - you can't help but notice gaggles of girls perfectly position their plates to get that all important insta pic. Open for breakfast, lunch and dinner (as well as sweet treats in between) the food selection prides itself on being natural, largely plant-based and always sourced in a socially and environmentally responsible way. Should you venture here for a meal, we recommend you try 'The MaE Bowl' which allows you to choose any four of the dishes to go inside. Though the selection on offer makes this decision difficult, the fast-forming queue behind you leaves no time for mouth-watering indecision. When you're done, finish off the meal with a healthy matcha latte and a cheeky peanut butter slice ... #maedelicious

MAPLE & FITZ

36A BERNERS STREET, FITZROVIA, W1T 3LY

OPEN

MON-FRI.   8:00AM - 4:00PM
SAT-SUN.   CLOSED

 MAPLEANDFITZ.COM

 GOODGE STREET

This cute little café is a great option for a quick and healthy breakfast bite or a grab n' go lunch. If you're looking for a reason to get out of bed in the morning, the Avocado Chilli Toast here is just that. With a very small seating area at the front of the shop, Maple & Fitz cater to those time-poor, health savvy workers who need tasty food to eat on the move or back at their desk. The grain bowls and salads change with the seasons and the cold-pressed juices are all made in-house.

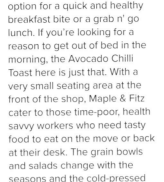

For those looking for a cool refreshing cuppa, they also sell organic, Fairtrade CHARitea iced tea in their fridge... a great chance to drink responsibly!

THE NATURAL KITCHEN

77 - 78 MARYLEBONE HIGH STREET, MARYLEBONE, W1U 5JX

OPEN

MON-FRI.   7:00AM - 8:00PM
SAT.   8:00AM - 7:00PM
SUN.   9:00AM - 7:00PM

 THENATURALKITCHEN.COM

 BAKER STREET

Anything with the word 'natural' in gets us excited, and the Natural Kitchen on Marylebone High Street doesn't disappoint. This restaurant/deli concept prides itself on sourcing local ingredients - essential for those of us looking to cut down the carbon footprint. The market fish and seafood here is particularly good, as is the healthy salads section of the menu. The pulses and beans that fill out the salads take them out of that 'plain, boring salad' box and make them a nutritious option for a light lunch. The large seating area means that although this is

a popular option for a tasty work lunch, it's usually possible to get a table without the wait. Check out the food to go deli before you leave - why not pickup dinner while you're there?

NEAL'S YARD PRIDE KITCHEN

2 NEAL'S YARD, COVENT GARDEN, WC2H 9DP

OPEN

MON-FRI.   9:00AM - 5:00PM

SAT-SUN.   9:00AM - 6:00PM

🌐 SALADPRIDE.COM

⊖ COVENT GARDEN

Neal's Yard Pride Kitchen (formally Saladpride), was born out of the lunch box of David Bez, a self-proclaimed Italian food lover and a man that has sexed up salads. This delightful little eatery (by little we literally mean one communal table that fits about 8 people) is a delicious edition to Neal's Yard in Covent Garden. With a real 'roots of the earth' vibe, the menu is entirely vegan, using pulses and grains to create filling and nutritious meals. The creative use of vegetables, raw flavours and edible flowers offers a vibrant taste experience that's designed to please the eyes as well as the palette - get your iPhones at the ready. The Red Velvet Beetroot Latte here is certainly one to write home about, unique in taste, texture and the exciting tint of pink! The organic food selection, topped off with an impressive choice of pukka tea and healthy hot drinks, makes this place a mecca for the wellness tribe.

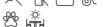

FOOD CAFÉS, DELIS + FOOD TO GO

PETERSHAM NURSERIES CAFÉ

PETERSHAM ROAD, RICHMOND, TW10 7AG

OPEN

MON.	CLOSED
TUE-FRI.	12:00PM - 2:00PM
SAT-SUN.	12.00PM - 3.30PM

🌐 PETERSHAMNURSERIES.COM

🚇 RICHMOND

Forget West London, Petersham Nurseries is one of the most romantic destinations in the UK. Five minutes from Petersham along a dirt track, you'll turn into the plot of land that bears the garden shop, a glass covered teahouse, and Petersham Nurseries Café; a restaurant and retail area contained in the main building. Here, green plants tumble from ceiling-height grids, and flowers in their vibrant variations dominate from start to finish, contained in majestic Grecian pots. The space is of Shakespeare's Midsummer Night's Dream ilk; paintings of what seem to be old Indian maharajas add to that far-off, slightly dreamy feel. The bar is set up on a cart, with all sorts of fascinating concoctions available, and the menu is inspired by Italy. As Petersham Nurseries is owned by the Boglione family, it is fitting that the constantly evolving menu should be motivated by Italian flavour, what's growing in the garden, and what's in season. Petersham Nurseries holds a host of events, from wine tasting, to gardening masterclasses. Escape here for a chance to unwind - bring your partner, your parent or just your pooch for a calming cup of whole leaf tea and a homemade slice of quiche.

PROTEIN HAUS

MOORGATE STATION, MOORGATE, EC2M 6TX

OPEN

MON-FRI.   6:30AM - 9:00PM
SAT.   10:00AM - 7:00PM
SUN.   12:00PM - 6:00PM

 PROTEINHAUS.CO.UK

 MOORGATE

Hotly rumoured to serve the best protein shakes in London, Protein Haus occupies a grab n' go space inside Moorgate Station. Established to help time-poor Londoners achieve their wellbeing goals, services include everything from take-out protein shakes and fitness food. Here, protein shakes are made to your spec, freshly prepared detox juices are ready to go, coffee contains protein, and there is an array of boxed-up lean meals and seed-rich snacks to choose from. Where healthy eating normally goes hand in hand with laborious preparation, Protein Haus cleverly offers

fast, knowledgeable, nutritious solutions, for the savviest of clean eaters. Whether you're after a comprehensive lifestyle approach, or just an energy-packed green juice to see you on your way, this health haven is a forward-thinking venue in a convenient location.

RAWLIGION

3 TOTTENHAM STREET, FITZROVIA, W1T 2AF

OPEN

MON-FRI.   7:30AM - 7:00PM
SAT.   10:00AM - 6:00PM
SUN.   CLOSED

 RAWLIGION.CO.UK

 GOODGE STREET

True to its name, Rawligion is a sacred spot that serves only organic plant-based, vegan food. With no preservatives in sight, this place is a haven for anyone seeking out something fresh and raw. The décor of the café is earth-inspired, with real viridian moss covering the wall behind the bar. There is a small seating area toward the back of this fast-casual café that's enshrined with ivy and hanging lamps; a celestial touch to this furtive garden spot. While Rawligion prides itself on being free from gluten and dairy, the selection of botanical drinks, raw chocolates and cauliflower sushi thankfully avoid the risk of being free from flavour. The owner

John Tabatabai, is often on hand to share his passion about the power of plant-based food and he's known to offer tasters to the curious customer. The dairy-free Brain Boosting Milk is a best seller, but if you're looking for something more hardcore, Poseidon's Trident (fennel, lime, sugar kelp, sea salt, chlorophyll) should hit the spot.

RUDE HEALTH

212 NEW KING'S ROAD, FULHAM, SW6 4NZ

OPEN

MON-SUN.   8:00AM - 5:00PM

 RUDEHEALTH.COM

 PUTNEY BRIDGE

It's impossible to miss this jazzy little café, at the very end of the New King's Road (toward Putney Bridge), its bright orange exterior, lime green shutters and funky blue tables undoubtedly catch the attention of any passer-by. Opened in 2015 by husband and wife team Camilla and Nick Barnard, the Rude Health brand began with an initial range of muesli in 2005, so it's no surprise that this place is best visited for its breakfast selection. Serving porridges, cereals, granolas, snack bars, dairy-free drinks as well as a small offering of seasonal salads and sandwiches for lunch; Rude Health Café has a keen focus on dishes that are natural and nutrient-rich. With large glass-fronted windows and Wi-Fi, this is a fantastic spot to get some out of office work done - nothing like a bowl of porridge topped with blueberries, mascarpone and maple seeds to keep the concentration levels up! Equally, the large tables make it a fitting spot for friends to gather over a turmeric latte and plan their next keepfit class... it would be rude not to!

OPEN

MON-FRI.   7:30AM - 9:00PM
SAT-SUN.   CLOSED

 SIMPLEHEALTHKITCHEN.COM

 MANSION HOUSE /
CANNON STREET

SIMPLE HEALTH KITCHEN

73A WATLING STREET, THE CITY, EC4M 9BJ

At Simple Health Kitchen, ingredients are everything - and everywhere. The cratefulls of vegetables proudly on display behind the counter, framed images of spinach, kale, carrots and intriguing vases of different shapes filled to their brims with seeds and pulps. With a colour palette of healthy apricot and pure white, it's obvious that this eatery is a place of wellbeing. The Super Berry juice, freshly made up of strawberry, blueberry, raspberry, banana, blackberry and blackcurrant is full of antioxidants, and Dr Detox is a delicious way to cleanse after a wild weekend. If you're yearning for a treat though, the kitchen's homemade 'raw snickers' and 'raw bounty' bars pack all the flavour of old classics, without defying squats, sit-ups or burpees. Natural ingredients and an entirely handmade approach mean that breakfast and lunch is an array of goodness. Spacious seating, sink-in couches and a breakfast bar with peach and white stools (and available plugs) make this an ideal venue to come for lunch with colleagues.

TINY LEAF

MERCATO METROPOLITANO, 42 NEWINGTON CAUSEWAY, ELEPHANT AND CASTLE, SE1 6DR

OPEN

MON.   CLOSED

TUE-SUN.   11:00AM - 11:00PM

🌐 TINYLEAFLONDON.COM

⊖ ELEPHANT AND CASTLE / BOROUGH

If you haven't already been to Mercato Metropolitano food market in Borough, then now is the time to go. Tiny Leaf - London's first organic, zero waste, vegetarian pop-up - has set up shop and made this its humble abode. Weave your way through the stalls to find Tiny Leaf serving vegan, vegetarian and gluten-free food for breakfast, lunch and dinner. The menu is constructed from organic surplus produce that is supplied by local food suppliers, supermarkets, farms, distributors, plant breeders and retailers. At its core, Tiny Leaf

is taking a sustainable step toward cutting out unnecessary wastage, whether that's by getting the most from misshapen vegetables, ignoring superficial damage to packaging or simply adding the skins to the broth instead of throwing them away.

TIOSK

33 BROADWAY MARKET, SOUTH HACKNEY, E8 4PH

OPEN

MON-FRI.   9:30AM - 5:00PM

SAT-SUN.   9:30AM - 6:00PM

🌐 TIOSK.CO.UK

⊖ BETHNAL GREEN

This delightful little shop and tea bar is East London at its finest. With large widows and exposed brick walls painted a muted brown, copper piping connects the lightbulbs adding a subtle industrial edge. The warmly lit interior compliments the warming drinks. Not only do they serve super infusions, blends and botanics, but they also serve green, black and white tea, iced tea and lattes. For anyone trying to teatox, TIOSK is the place to come. Experiment with the Super sunshine latte or the Moroccan mint blend to switch up your usual Earl Grey. If you're looking for food, on the house

menu you'll find dishes like Smashed avocado with pumpkin seeds and Juniper smoked salmon with wasabi diffused mayonnaise, fresh dill and rocket, ideal for a brunch date. Impress your mum with a gift of her favourite loose-leaf tea.

VITA MOJO

22 CARTER LANE, THE CITY, EC4V 5AD

OPEN

MON-FRI. 7:00AM - 9:00PM
SAT-SUN. CLOSED

 VITAMOJO.COM

 ST PAUL'S

Vita Mojo is the future of fast food. Just a short walk from St Paul's tube station, you'll love how quick and convenient it is to pick and personalise your meal. Set out on an iPad, you're presented with a variety of ingredients such as: sweet potato mash, broccoli, red cabbage, kale salad or grilled Atlantic salmon and you simply adjust the quantity of each to suit your own dietary needs and appetite. This method of ultra-personalization allows people to see and control exactly what they put in to their bodies (no hidden sugars, fats or calories). It's a Godsend

for anyone with difficult food allergies or intolerances and makes watching what you eat that much easier. The design of the shop focuses on natural goodness, with live moss displayed on one wall and plant baskets hanging from above.

WILD FOOD CAFÉ

1ST FLOOR, 14 NEAL'S YARD, COVENT GARDEN, WC2H 9DP

OPEN

MON. CLOSED
TUE-THU. 11:30AM - 9:00PM
FRI-SAT. 11:30AM - 10:00PM
SUN. 11:30AM - 7:00PM

 WILDFOODCAFE.COM

 COVENT GARDEN

You can't miss it - it's not possible. Nestled into eclectic Covent Garden hangout, Neal's Yard, Wild Food Café is an array of colour; windows and door frames painted in blues, greens and yellows, with a gigantic orange sign, all set off by their red brick building. That's just a taster of the vibrant cooking going on inside. The global food served up is fresh and colourful, with a curated, gourmet twist; all sourced from small organic farmers, ethical local suppliers, or foraged from pristine ecosystems. Communal wooden tables and benches establish the friendly, social ambience,

ready for the celebration of plant food due to arrive. The menu is based on seasonal ingredients, constantly evolving depending on what's available. Order the Wild Burger for a taste of the savoury rainbow.

NATURALLY SASSY'S GUIDE TO BUILDING A SUCCESSFUL BLOG IN THE WORLD OF WELLNESS

BY **SASKIA GREGSON-WILLIAMS**

My blog is how I built my brand. I'm a cookery writer, author and creator of Ballet Blast, a fitness method that fuses high intensity training with classical dance principles.

With a background as a ballet dancer, training up to 8 hours a day, I learnt the importance of food and the power it has to make us feel and look our best. However, the ballet world is full of conflicting messages and for the best part of my teenage years I used food not as fuel but to help me strive for the stereotypical ballerina aesthetic. Those years were miserable and I found that conforming to an industry ideal was not healthy for my body or mind - this is what sparked the idea of starting a blog. I learnt I had a real passion and flair in the kitchen and over time this grew into an overwhelming desire to share the food I was creating, in the hope that it would get other young women cooking good food from scratch too. The success of my blog was very unexpected, with tens of thousands of page reads in the first few months. I knew there was an audience here, and one I wanted to continue to reach out to, inspiring them to love the skin they're in through great-tasting food as well as butt-lifting movement through my Ballet Blast. A simple idea snowballed into many outside projects, including a cookbook, limited edition energy bar range and many exciting collaborative ventures.

When I started my blog I knew very little about blogging, but a few years on, it seems everybody has one. It's a harder craft, and creating exciting original content is more important than ever. But, how to get started? That's the most important part. As much as I wish I could say that content is everything, I don't believe it is. A huge part of the puzzle is presentation and this is where web design comes in. To build a successful blog you have to have a good platform to begin with, and whilst bespoke-original website designs can be awfully expensive for a first-time blogger, there are ways to create a unique online space for slightly less. There are thousands of Wordpress templates online that you can buy and build the website into - shop around and find one that suits your style. Now, find a good web designer to help build your content into the template or give it a go yourself! If you opt for the latter, hunt instead for a graphic designer and get a solid logo under your belt. Pick a colour scheme and stick to it - everything about your content should be memorable. Photography is another key area - invest in a good camera, watch video tutorials and find your own way.

You've built your platform, but now it's time to think about that stand-out content you're going fill it with. The two most important elements to consider are, (1) what are you most passionate about? (2) what will the readers gain from it? Making sure your readers will come away with something is key. Are you offering knowledge? Advice? A good old laugh at the end of a hard day? Know what you'll be giving them to keep them visiting time and time again.

You've got a fully-fledged blog, and now you need to get the flocks flying your way. Social media is key to creating a loyal online readership. Create consistent content on your Instagram and get involved in relevant conversations on Twitter, building your online presence. I find Instagram to be the best media for visual content, recipes and photography, while Twitter is good for connecting with individuals.

Reach out to likeminded brands and offer your expertise, or propose a relevant collaboration. This could be an event, reviewing their product or donating an article to their blog. Whatever it may be, creating genuine relationships within your sector is incredibly important. From here you may be invited to an event and gain the opportunity to meet many other bloggers and brands in your field. One big mistake a lot of beginner bloggers make is thinking the key to a successful blog is all online, but like most jobs there's nothing like connecting with people face to face. Take every opportunity you have to attend an event, as you never know what it may lead to.

The continuous struggle for a blogger is creating new content. With so many different articles covering a broad range of topics being published every day it's easy to feel like you're starting to mimic somebody else. Keeping your individual voice and creating something different is the only way to continue to grow. When I'm stuck for ideas I use three different approaches to gain inspiration. The first is reaching out to my audience and asking what they'd like to see. This is often a recipe for something chocolatey (I have a pretty predictable readership) or a new home workout. The second approach is to look at my favourite publications content from 5-10 years ago. Some of the features that we don't see anymore are great to inspire new ideas for your own content. The third route I use for inspiration is simply looking to myself and thinking what I would like to read if I was a Naturally Sassy reader. Taking myself out of the head of the creator and into the mind of the reader always insights new ideas.

When it comes to creating new recipes I generally look to old favourites for inspiration. I love re-creating the more indulgent meals I grew up adoring. I'll flick through baking books or drool at Italian feasts, finding what I'd love to re-create in a healthier manner. Seasonal food and different cuisines also inspire me, I can't get out of the kitchen after a trip abroad, I come back home with far too many ideas. To set your food apart, be a real stickler for quality. Perfect a recipe before you publish

and spend time over writing up the easiest most efficient cooking method. Work on your food styling, and be consistent with your photography style. There are so many elements that will set your food apart, beyond the simple flavours.

As the trends change in your line of blogging it's important you always stay true to the voice that started the blog in the first place. You can grow and change, but being open about this and not compromising yourself for what you think people want to see is the best piece of advice I can give you. Nothing is more attractive than genuine, passionate content, and that always shines through.

OPEN

MON–FRI.	8:00AM – 10:00PM
SAT.	11:30AM – 10:00PM
SUN.	10:00AM – 4:00PM

 ETHOSFOODS.COM

 OXFORD CIRCUS

ETHOS

48 EASTCASTLE STREET, FITZROVIA, W1W 8DX

This buffet style vegetarian restaurant is both a feast for the eyes and the stomach. Prepare to test your self-restraint with its pay-by-weight concept that charges based on the amount of food you've managed to pile upon your plate. This central London-based garden of Eden, with its extensive selection of gluten-free, dairy-free and vegan options, shows how a little creativity can lead to a lot of great flavour. Set up by Jessica Kruger to share the deliciousness of meat-free food, this uber-trendy spot pulls in an impressive crowd for lunch and dinner. The mixture of hot and cold dishes, ranging from Japanese miso aubergine to artichoke stuffed potato bites and massaged kale salad with kumquats, is inspired by cuisine from around the world, leading you on a voyage of taste discovery. Soak in the Nordic feel of this restaurant, with tree trunks gathered between the tables, it's the textbook venue for any tasty teddy bear's picnic!

FARMACY

74 WESTBOURNE GROVE, NOTTING HILL, W2 5SH

OPEN

MON-FRI.	8:00AM - 11:00PM
SAT.	12:00PM - 11:00PM
SUN.	10:00AM - 7:00PM

 FARMACYLONDON.COM

 BAYSWATER / ROYAL OAK

The gold bar at the centre of this cult Notting Hill restaurant is a mark of standard. Apothecary bottles line the top shelf alongside dainty pot plants. Dining at Farmacy is an experience as good as they come, built around raw curated food and beautiful design. Stepping outside of the realm of French-style brasseries, green food cafés and wholefoods stores, this is the real deal. The vegetarian food is as fresh and inspired as the design. Cashew cheese and almond milk are prepared from scratch every morning by the chefs in their smart green pinstriped aprons and every ingredient here is organic and carefully sourced - the quality speaks for itself. Brunch at Farmacy is simply not to be missed; the avocado on toast and house pancakes are obvious hits, while the Eggs Florentine showcase what Farmacy is really about. Did we mention that the Hollandaise sauce is made from carrots, thyme and cider vinegar? Here, healthy food isn't restrictive; it's adventurous and creative, with flavour that keeps you on your toes. Although the main menu changes in line with the season every 3 months, thankfully, the Farmacy Burger will always remain. Dubbed one of the best vegan burgers in the world, its black bean and millet patty is well worth a journey.

ITADAKI ZEN

139 KING'S CROSS ROAD, KING'S CROSS, WC1X 9BJ

OPEN

MON-SAT.	12:00PM - 2:30PM |
	6:00PM - 9:45PM
SUN.	CLOSED

 ITADAKIZEN-UK.COM

 KING'S CROSS

Officially accredited as one of London's most authentic Japanese restaurants, Itadaki Zen stands out from the crowd in offering exclusively organic vegan food. Using Asian-inspired ingredients such as noodles, seaweed sushi and tofu, with the addition of seasonal vegetables, they serve a tasty combination of flavours and textures mainly in set menus. Their adaptation of the Japanese cuisine to work in the absence of fish, meat and dairy is a creative feat; instead they ensure the food is flavoured with oriental herbs, wild plants and delicate dressing. The restaurant is small, but you'll notice that both the décor and the food are authentic to their Japanese origins. With wooden tables, beams and chairs, the traditional memorabilia on show inspire a visual and a culinary journey to Japan.

LA SUITE WEST RAW

45 - 51 INVERNESS TERRACE, BAYSWATER, W2 3JN

OPEN

MON-SUN.	6:30AM - 9:00PM

 LASUITEWEST.COM

QUEENSWAY

Located in the nirvana of whitewashed brick that is Inverness Terrace, this contemporary restaurant resides within La Suite West Hotel. True to its name, RAW serves a selection of vegan-friendly, dairy-free and raw dishes. Chef Nik Heartland designed the menu to provide the best that nature can offer and then showcase it at its finest. The 50-seat restaurant is small, sleek and minimally designed, with black tables, chairs and mirrors. From courgetti - a dish of spiralized courgette with sunflower seed pesto, tomato and red pepper ragout - to aubergine involtini, the main menu is rooted in a contemporary Mediterranean cooking style. RAW work hard so that you don't have to compromise taste for health, offering both traditional vegan dishes and completely new ones. No plans after lunch? They offer a delicious vegan Afternoon Tea.

MANNA

4 ERSKINE ROAD, PRIMROSE HILL, NW3 3AJ

OPEN

MON.	CLOSED
TUE-FRI.	12:00PM - 3:00PM |
	6:30PM - 10:00PM
SAT.	12:00PM - 3:00PM |
	6:00PM - 10:00PM
SUN.	12:00PM - 7:30PM

 MANNAV.COM

 CHALK FARM

Who would have thought that a vegan restaurant would be most famous for its bangers and mash? Well, Manna is. Not just that, but the Primrose Hill restaurant is a regular celebrity haunt and arguably one of the most well known vegan outlets in London. This is no slap and dash café; it's a gourmet restaurant, which has established a strong presence over fifty years (initially a vegetarian restaurant, coming into the hands of its new owners in 1995, and now 100% vegan). The team aim to offer nourishing, delicious food, in a friendly and relaxed environment with expert service. Basil cashew cheese croquettes are an indulgent starter, winking back at childhood, and the famous organic bangers and mash are curated with masterful flair; sausages of organic fennel and pumpkin seeds, seasonal greens, garlic potato, dill and carrot mash, leek and thyme jus and onion rings. If you fancy something lighter, opt for the cold soba noodle salad; a fresh concoction of buckwheat noodles, seasonal vegetables and peanut chilli dressing. For dessert? Pick cheesecake every time - an evolving daily special, you'll be full to bursting by the end.

MILDREDS

45 LEXINGTON STREET, SOHO, W1F 9AN

OPEN

MON-SAT.   12:00PM - 11:00PM

SUN.   CLOSED

 MILDREDS.CO.UK

OXFORD CIRCUS /
PICCADILLY CIRCUS

This vegetarian and vegan hotspot is an oasis of goodness, from the virtuous green hanging garden at its centre, to friendly staff and nourishing food, made daily on site. Located on Lexington Street in an 18th Century townhouse, the restaurant's sterling reputation means it is regularly packed out (it's no bookings policy gives you the perfect excuse to enjoy an impromptu cocktail whilst you wait). For a quick lunch, head for the take away bar, which offers up fresh salads, soup, quiche and daily specials at great prices. For a sit down meal, Soul Bowl (a duo of superfood salads) and Detox Salad (a sweet and tangy concoction) are sure to get your metabolism going and boost your immune system. But if it's something hot you're after, try Sri Lankan sweet potato and green bean curry. With roasted lime cashews, pea basmati rice and coconut tomato sambal, it's a gorgeous and nutritious combination; but the burgers are admittedly hard to pass on. Luckily, they, too, are health-conscious, based on either tofu, halloumi or beetroot.

PALM VAULTS

411 MARE STREET, HACKNEY, E8 1HY

OPEN

MON.	CLOSED
TUE-SUN.	8:00AM - 5:30PM

 PALMVAULTS.COM

 HACKNEY CENTRAL RAIL

A short walk from Hackney Central, this eatery offers up a moment outside of time. Arguably one of London's most Instagramable brunch spots, the interiors marry 80s Americana with an industrial East End London edge. The design is resolutely pink (albeit with a dash of sea green), from the marble tables and leather chairs, down to the water jugs and receipts. Palm Vaults has a homemade-from-scratch policy, ranging from freshly-made juices, health shots (try charcoal and ginger for a morning zing), to smoothies

and homemade health lattes (try velvet or lavender). They serve waffles and pancakes made from buckwheat, bespoke smoothie bowls and vegan soft serve ice cream (available in the summer). Beware of the brain freeze!

TIBITS

12 - 14 HEDDON STREET, MAYFAIR, W1B 4DA

OPEN

MON-WED.	9:00AM - 10:30PM
THU-SAT.	9:00AM - 12:00AM
SUN.	11:30AM - 10:30PM

 TIBITS.CO.UK

 OXFORD CIRCUS / PICCADILLY CIRCUS

On Tuesdays we go vegan - or at least that's the case at Tibits. Though every other day, the menu is vegetarian. This small Swiss chain, with its seasonally inspired menus, can be found just off Regent's street. Laid out in a 'food boat' the buffet concept allows you to mix and match the dishes of your choice. Offering breakfast, lunch and dinner, you're charged by the weight of your plate - so keep that in mind when you're piling on the potatoes. The restaurant has a casual, modern feel. An easy option for a speedy lunch stop.

VANILLA BLACK

17 - 18 TOOK'S COURT, CHANCERY LANE, EC4A 1LB

OPEN

MON-SAT.   12:00PM - 2:30PM |
                6:00PM - 10:00PM
SUN.   CLOSED

 VANILLABLACK.CO.UK

 CHANCERY LANE

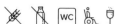

Located just off Chancery Lane, Vanilla Black serves innovative vegetarian food to the smartly dressed suits that saunter through. This fine-dining restaurant is the co-creation of Andrew Dargue (head chef) and partner Donna Conroy. They believe the fact that it's vegetarian is 'neither here nor there' as the priority is to create dishes that are delicious, unusual and forward thinking in their desire to push the culinary boundaries. Using the fact that it's meat-free to be more experimental and creative, the dishes change with the seasons but stay rooted in

their English and French classical style of cooking - with a twist. The wooden floors feel rustic, but the visually stunning design of the food looks contemporary. While many might shun the idea of a meatless meal, eating here is no missed steak!

VITAO

25 - 27 OXFORD STREET, SOHO, W1D 2DW

OPEN

MON-SAT.   11:00AM - 11:00PM
SUN.   11:00AM - 9:00PM

 VITAO.CO.UK

TOTTENHAM COURT ROAD

While certainly not the most glamorous restaurant in town, Vitao is a vegan eatery that serves up an interesting variety of free-from dishes. Easy to miss given its location right next to the hustle and bustle of Tottenham Court Road tube station, the vegan buffet here is a fun find and open from late morning to late evening. With dishes that change daily, Vitao offers a fine selection of stews, soups, grilled vegetables and grain-based salads. Though, the pay-by-weight system means that attempting to fit too many of these multi-ethnic options on your plate may result

in a hefty bill, as well as an overpowering combination of tastes and flavours. This place is best regarded for its raw and steamed desserts, the Raw Blueberry Fudge Cake is a real delight. Treat yourself to a warm cup of herbal tea on the side.

ADVICE FOR EATING HEALTHILY ON A BUDGET

AN INTERVIEW WITH MADELEINE SHAW BY THE LONDON WELLNESS GUIDE

Madeleine is a nutritional health coach, qualified yoga instructor, bestselling cookery writer and creator of the Glow Guides app. Her philosophy is simple: ditch the junk and eat your way to a healthy lifestyle that is both sustainable and delicious. She cooks with wholefoods, meat, fish and plenty of flavour, and is a strong advocate for focusing on the good stuff, rather than beating yourself up about the bad.

What advice would you give to people who want to eat healthily on a budget?

Cook once, eat twice. Whip up a nice, big pot of curry or stew on a Sunday night and this can be used again for lunch the next day. Make things easy for yourself and freeze whatever is left. This means you'll have ready-made portions for later in the week. Preparation is key when it comes to eating healthily because buying out can get so expensive!

I also love to eat seasonally. Not only is seasonal produce fresh and readily available, but it's much cheaper and tends to taste better. Cut down your carbon footprint as well as your cost when you buy food that is locally sourced. My new book, A Year of Beautiful Eating, focuses on using wonderful, in season ingredients to make delicious meals!

What are the essential ingredients that you always have available?

Coconut oil, eggs and porridge oats are staples that can always be found somewhere in my cupboard. These are my top 3 because there is so just so much you can do with them. Porridge oats will always fill you up and coconut oil adds flavour to anything. The possibilities with eggs are simply endless.

Where do you find inspiration for a new dish?

I love collecting menus - my collection is constantly expanding. Eating out inspires me to experiment at home. I try to recreate unusual flavour combinations that tasted good and at the same time I always think, 'how I can add my own twist to make this taste even better?'. That's why cooking is so fun, it's all about playing around with tastes, textures and deliciousness.

Some healthy eating recipes can be flavourless; how do you ensure your recipes are delicious and inspiring? - any secret ingredients?

I love that we've moved away from this idea that healthy eating simply means salad with no side dressing! There is so much you can do with fresh, natural food eaten in moderation. I can't stand a bland dish, so Asian-inspired ingredients like ginger, chilli and tamari (soy sauce) are always useful. A little bit of these can turn a boring recipe into something totally dreamy!

If you don't have time to cook, where is your favourite place to eat?

For breakfast, brunch, lunch or dinner? Nowadays, I feel spoilt for choice. London's gastronomic scene is constantly exploding with delicious places to eat out and on the go. There are so many amazing places to choose from, but I genuinely love my boyfriend's restaurant Boma, there is something for everyone and it has an amazing brunch menu.

TWO SPRING LUNCH BOXES

These fresh lunch boxes are as wonderfully colourful as they are tasty. With lots of luscious crunchy veggies, why not team them together for a super lunch box?

BUCKWHEAT TABBOULEH WITH ROCKET, RADISHES AND SPRING ONION

Serves 1

70g cooked buckwheat
1 tomato, diced
¼ cucumber, diced
50g rocket
4 radishes, sliced
1 spring onion, finely chopped
2 tbsp chopped fresh coriander
Salt and freshly ground black pepper, to taste
1 tbsp olive oil
Juice of ½ lemon

Put the buckwheat and veggies together in a lunch container. Sprinkle on the coriander and season with a big pinch of salt and pepper and mix well.

Keep in the fridge until lunchtime, then pour over the oil and lemon juice just before eating.

PRAWN, GRAPEFRUIT AND AVOCADO SALAD

Serves 1

1 little gem lettuce, sliced
½ grapefruit, peeled and sliced
150g cooked prawns
½ avocado, pitted, peeled and sliced
1 tbsp olive oil
1 tsp freshly grated ginger
juice of ½ lime
½ red chilli, deseeded and finely chopped

Mix the lettuce, grapefruit, prawns and avocado together in your lunch box.

Whisk the oil, ginger, lime and chilli together, and pour on top of your salad.

Keep in the fridge until lunchtime.

OPEN

MON-SUN.   11:30AM - 9:00PM

 AHIPOKE.CO.UK

TOTTENHAM COURT ROAD

AHI POKÉ

3 PERCY STREET, FITZROVIA, W1T 1DF

With white-washed floorboards and exposed brick walls, sanded pinewood tables and bright tones of blue on the tiled counter, Ahi Poké replicates a small slice of the sunny Pacific for hungry Londoners. This build-your-bowl concept is popular amongst the urban healthies as it allows you to see exactly what makes up your meal. The signature bowls; 'Sweet Green', 'Heat Wave', 'Oahu' and 'Venice' reflect the Hawaiian vibe with an added Asian fusion. Simple and quick, you pick your base, add your fish and mushroom, choose your sauce and mix in a topping. Served in see-through bowls, the colourful combination of fresh ingredients makes this an Insta-winner. Well placed on a wooden surfboard is a fluorescent neon sign that jests, 'You've just been pokéd' - a reminder that healthy food can be fun and they're bringing poké to the people! The glass-fronted store seats around 16 but given its location so close to Tottenham Court Road, it's also a great grab n' go option for busy shoppers.

OPEN

MON–FRI.	8:00AM –11:30PM
SAT.	10:00AM - 11:30PM
SUN.	10:00AM - 4:00PM

🌐 CARAVANRESTAURANTS.CO.UK

⊖ KING'S CROSS

CARAVAN

1 GRANARY SQUARE, KING'S CROSS, N1C 4AA

While Caravan King's Cross might not be considered your stereotypical health and wellness hotspot, the seasonally inspired menu has plenty to get you glowing. The industrial chic interior of this restaurant has a wonderfully chilled out vibe, despite the caffeinated buzz from its organic, in-house coffee roastery. Clearly the lively, arty crowd delight in the lively, arty food! With a natural light that floods through the large window, the fresh vegetables stand to attention; the stark pink of the beetroot, the vibrant orange of the shredded carrot and the deep green of the stem broccoli. The pick-and-mix style here is a great option for sharing. To get a real feel for the variety of flavours, combine a number of the small plates. Be sure to ask for the server's recommendations and if it sounds delicious on the menu, it's even better served up in front of you.

FARM GIRL

59A PORTOBELLO ROAD, NOTTING HILL, W11 3DB

OPEN

MON-FRI.	8:30AM - 4:30PM
SAT.	9:00AM - 5:00PM
SUN.	9:00AM - 4:00PM

🌐 THEFARMGIRL.CO.UK

🚇 NOTTING HILL GATE

A subtle turning off the Portobello Road will lead you into a cosy courtyard where the Farm Girl Café awaits. They don't take reservations so prepare to meet queues before quinoa (but don't let this put you off!). Farm Girl was set up by hard-working couple, Rose Mann and Anthony Wood, who have injected their Aussie penchant for fresh and delicious produce. First impressions will tell you that this is where fashion meets feel-great food, there's good taste in every sense. With its stylish set up, it's a try before you die for lifestyle bloggers across London. Anyone looking for the latest in adventurous options, Farm Girl fits the bill. The Latte Black (a double shot blended with activated charcoal and date syrup) and the Liquid Gold Latte (turmeric, cinnamon, astragalus, honey and coconut milk) are sought after specialties. Ranging from berry pancakes to white Devon crab cakes, it's good to know the reputation that precedes this eatery does not let it down.

FARMSTAND

42 DRURY LANE, COVENT GARDEN, WC2B 5AJ

OPEN

MON-FRI.	7:30AM - 9:00PM
SAT.	9:00AM - 9:00PM
SUN.	CLOSED

🌐 FARMSTAND.CO.UK

🚇 COVENT GARDEN

If you're scouting out West End superstars, then you've come to the right place. We're not just talking about the harissa chicken or the roasted sweet potatoes, ginger and coconut yogurt side dish (OMG), we're also talking about the stage performers that discreetly swing by to grab their pre-show dinner. Found on Drury lane, the heart of London's theatreland, Farmstand fuses industrial chic with lush green potted plants - it's urban edgy with a natural twist. Opened in 2016, the menu changes every four months (in line with the seasons) but stays completely dairy, refined sugar and gluten free, and the majority of the side dishes are vegan. Ingredients are sourced solely from farms around the UK but there's no holding back when it comes to the flavourful combinations. Lunchtime gets busy, but with an abundance of seating both upstairs and down, you need not worry. This is a fabulous find if you're looking to retreat from the cobbled streets of Covent Garden or meet a friend before that sell-out show. They also serve organic, gluten-free lager! Hakuna Matata to that.

THE GATE

51 QUEEN CAROLINE STREET, HAMMERSMITH, W6 9QL

OPEN

MON-FRI.	12:00PM - 2:00PM | 6:00PM - 10:00PM
SAT.	12:00PM - 2:30PM | 5:00PM - 10:00PM
SUN.	12:00AM - 9:15PM

 THEGATERESTAURANTS.COM

 HAMMERSMITH

Found on Queen Caroline Street, the understated entrance to The Gate Hammersmith makes it feel like a well-hidden secret. What was once the studio of artist Sir Frank Brangwyn is now a large, lofty dining room with wonderfully well-designed windows. The menu is vegetarian, but the range of choice is far from limited. There is a flavourful variety of options that will please even the most fervent meat-eater among us. Though the menu changes seasonally in line with what's fresh and in full bloom, certain favourites like the aubergine schnitzel, the Wild mushroom risotto cake and the Butternut Rotolo don't seem to go out of fashion. One glimpse at the fruity cocktail list and you'll see why people 'go wild' for this place, it's legendary!

GRAIN STORE

GRANARY SQUARE, 1 - 3 STABLE STREET, KING'S CROSS, N1C 4AB

OPEN

MON-SAT.	10:00AM - 11:30PM
SUN.	10:30AM - 3:30PM

 GRAINSTORE.COM

 KING'S CROSS

Who would have thought King's Cross would undergo such a drastic facelift, but in recent years it's become a trendy urban hangout for North London's creative crowd. Grain Store in Granary Square falls into this category of cool. The restaurant has been converted from what used to be the old granary building and though it's not vegetarian, the menu is predominantly plant-based which means that vegetables take pride of place. Open for lunch and dinner, as well as weekend brunch, the eclectic menu has been inspired by chef Bruno Loubet's travels around the world, as well as his beloved vegetable patch. The dishes range in taste, design and ingredients but stay true to the love and appreciation of plants (whether raw, cooked, fermented, steamed, sprouted, pickled or smoked). The open kitchen at the centre of the restaurant is a hive of activity - watch the chefs work like busy bees to prep and serve the delicious, natural fare. You've got a treat in store.

GRANGER & CO.

175 WESTBOURNE GROVE, NOTTING HILL, W11 2SB

OPEN

MON-SAT.   7:00AM - 11:00PM

SUN.   8:00AM - 10:30PM

🌐 GRANGERANDCO.COM

⊖ NOTTING HILL GATE

If you want to get a seat at this prime Wesbourne eatery, you'll have to arrive early; a no-bookings policy and sterling reputation for beautiful food mean that it's consistently packed out. Granger & Co is the first UK outlet of Australian restaurateur and celebrity cookery book author, Bill Granger. The space is simply designed - light and open - and has a chilled-out, welcoming vibe. The restaurant is most highly renowned for its breakfast; from simple bites like toasted coconut bread with butter, to more exciting, global dishes, like 'fresh Aussie' jasmine tea hot smoked salmon, poached eggs, greens, avocado and cherry tomato. The relaxed atmosphere and inviting global cuisine with extensive healthy options make Granger & Co a great place to unwind. For dinner, try the shrimp burger with jalapeño mayo, shaved radish salad and sesame gochujang; and when it comes to dessert, the banana fritters, citrus caramel and honey ice cream are famous. Colourful, adventurous, and friendly, Granger & Co brings a breath of fresh Aussie air to London.

HALLY'S

60 NEW KING'S ROAD, FULHAM, SW6 4LS

OPEN

MON-SUN.   8:00AM - 6:00PM

 HALLYSLONDON.COM

 PARSONS GREEN

Stepping inside this Californian-inspired café, the hustle and bustle of London quickly disappears. With wooden tables and exposed brick painted white, it feels like there should be a sandy beach in view. Found instead just off Parson's Green, the brunch menu here is especially popular with the young professional crowd that hang around Fulham. The bright yellow bar stools inject a slice of sunshine whatever the weather, so it's no surprise that this place is in high demand on the weekends. Buggies and puppies are warmly welcomed and the ricotta pancakes with berries, fig, honey and crème fraîche are simply to squat for! If you're in the mood for something slightly adventurous, the butterflied sardines on multigrain toast with salsa verde, tomato & watercress tastes like a trip to the Mediterranean. There's no denying that this is the place to go if you're looking for a hearty dollop of wholesome indulgence. Serving homemade, fresh food, Hally's is now open for dinner on Friday and Saturday evenings, so get booking date night!

HONEY & CO.

25 WARREN STREET, FITZROVIA, W1T 5LZ

OPEN

MON-FRI.	8:00AM - 10:30PM
SAT.	9:30AM - 10:30PM
SUN.	CLOSED

🌐 HONEYANDCO.CO.UK

🚇 WARREN STREET /
GREAT PORTLAND STREET

Little blue tables underneath the awning jutting out from this Warren Street Middle Eastern gem strike a welcoming tone. The tiny, but packed out, eatery's interiors are simple as can be, but it's an endearing quality. An array of small, fresh mezze dishes invariably dot across every table, from mouthwatering sesame falafel with tahini, to marinated aubergine. At Honey & Co. the ethos is simple; a love for the food that owners Sarit Packer and Itamar Srulovich grew up eating. Street food, dishes from the kitchens of family and friends, and their own culinary fantasies. The married couple have created a homely, welcoming space on Warren Street that has unfailingly drawn crowds. Shelving that spans the length of the café hosts a variety of goodies, from different wines through to Climpson & Sons coffee. On the counter sits temptation; clusters of homemade cakes that constitute the perfect way to wind up your visit. If you're looking for something new, fresh and healthy, with an exciting, wholesome buzz to it, make Honey & Co. your next stop.

ISLANDPOKE.CO.UK

OXFORD CIRCUS /
PICCADILLY CIRCUS

ISLAND POKÉ

8 KINGLY STREET, SOHO, W1B 5PQ

James Gould-Porter first discovered poké when he was nine after a tennis tournament in Maui, Hawaii. Poké literally means to dice or slice, and its core element is raw seafood of brilliant quality, served with rice, fruit and vegetables. In 2016, after a series of popular market pop-ups, Island Poké opened on Kingly Street permanently, sharing the invigorating, zingy Hawaiian food with Londoners. Three house bowls and one special give suggestions, but you can 'base it', 'top it' and 'finish it' as you like. Try Classic Ahi (tuna), Yuzu Lomi Lomi (salmon) and Beet It (beetroot), with sushi or brown rice for a filling meal, or leafy greens for a lighter option. Top with pineapple or mango salsa, and other options include: edamame beans, sesame seeds and spring onion.

JAR KITCHEN

176 DRURY LANE, COVENT GARDEN, WC2B 5QF

OPEN

SUN-MON.   CLOSED

TUE-SAT.   11:00AM - 12:00AM

 JARKITCHEN.COM

 COVENT GARDEN

Nestled amongst the shops and businesses of Drury Lane, this sophisticated yet unassuming restaurant draws the eye with its regal, deep blue exterior, large street-front windows and inviting interior. Opened in 2015, Jar Kitchen offers an appetising menu of modern European food inspired by worldwide cuisine. The kitchen's renowned chefs create beautiful brunch, lunch and dinner plates using seasonal ingredients and operating a zero waste policy as much as possible. Jar Kitchen offers two or three course pre-theatre menus, A La Carte dining (don't miss the mixed grain salad, carrots, JK yoghurt, pomegranate and almonds), and a tantalising bottomless brunch where you can tuck into black-eyed beans on sourdough bread with Clarence Court poached eggs, optional pork belly, and a selection of perfectly paired drinks. As a member of the Sustainable Restaurant Association and with ingredients sourced locally, dine in the knowledge that local providers benefit with every moreish mouthful.

JUSUBROTHERS.COM

 BAYSWATER /
NOTTING HILL GATE

JUSU BROTHERS

147 - 149 WESTBOURNE GROVE, COVENT GARDEN, W11 2RS

In summer, the large windows on the front of this Notting Hill café are opened outwards; the sun floods in during the day, and word on the block is that sunset is unmissable. At any time of year, this white space is a lively vision of health and happiness, and Jusu Brothers' motto, 'remedy for the soul' rings true. Hanging plants fall from the ceiling into little nests, and climbing plants crawl up pillars; friends, couples and colleagues chat over their tables, tucking in eagerly. Opened in 2016, Jusu Brothers' ambition is to make healthy living as easy as possible, but they are determined not to force it upon people. To them, it should be enjoyable. In this vein, cohorts of freshly made health juices, raw protein shakes and health shots feature alongside beer and wine. The juices on offer are simple yet effective; try Green with Attitude for an invigorating spinach, celery and apple concoction. The menu, too, offers options suitable for every diet, from the classic chia breakfast pudding, to chicken sandwiches and vegan sushi. Jusu Brothers is, above all, light and refreshing.

LEGGERO

64 OLD COMPTON STREET, SOHO, W1D 4UQ

OPEN

MON-FRI.	12:00PM - 10:30PM
SAT.	11:00AM - 11:00PM
SUN.	11:00AM - 10:30PM

🌐 LEGGERO-LONDON.COM

⊖ LEICESTER SQUARE

Gluten-free Italian fare seems oxymoronic, but LEGGERO proves that anything is possible with a little polenta and a lot of love. What was once La Polenteria, a well known family restaurant in Soho, is now dubbed LEGGERO. In Italian this means 'light', and true to their name they serve appetisers, small plates and mains that are healthy, homemade and coeliac friendly. In amongst the gluten-free goodness, the homemade pasta and ravioli come highly recommended. The restaurant itself is small yet cosy, with a décor that's light and colourful to compliment the home cooked food. The open kitchen at the back gives you a glimpse behind the scenes, but if you can, grab a table by the huge front window - a prime spot for people watching.

M RAW VICTORIA STREET

ZIG ZAG BUILDING, 70 VICTORIA STREET, VICTORIA, SW1E 6SQ

OPEN

MON-FRI.	7:00AM - 12:00AM
SAT.	10:00AM - 12:00AM
SUN.	CLOSED

🌐 MRESTAURANTS.CO.UK

⊖ VICTORIA

There was a time when Victoria was simply an area to pass through, but with the likes of M Raw so conveniently placed just a short walk away from the station, this part of London is undoubtedly on the up. Fusing together M Raw, M Grill, M Wine and M Bar, M Restaurants opened at the start of 2016. To the benefit of anyone on a wheat-free diet, the RAW section is 100% gluten-free. Serving a combination of sashimi, tartares and tempura, followed by super bowls or bento boxes, it promises only natural ingredients, along with sustainable and ethically-sourced fish. The seating area is downstairs, and the dark panelling around gives it a polished, club-like atmosphere. Breakfast is also available here and we'd recommend the RAW juices as just the thing for a fresh start!

MANUKA KITCHEN

510 FULHAM ROAD, FULHAM, SW6 5NJ

OPEN

MON.	6:00PM - 10:00PM
TUE-THU.	12:00PM - 11:00PM
FRI-SAT.	10:00AM - 11:00PM
SUN.	10:00AM - 5:00PM

 MANUKAKITCHEN.CO.UK

 FULHAM BROADWAY

On weekends, people simply swarm to Manuka Kitchen. Serving modern European cuisine and situated to one side of Fulham Broadway, this brasserie has a distinctive buzz that delivers a truly memorable dining experience. The rustic wooden tables mixed with the urban design of the hanging steel lighting and the ability to peep in to the kitchen at the back, gives this place an effortless appearance of cool. Manuka's culinary creations here invoke a unique blend of flavours and taste sensations. The lemongrass and Manuka honey cured salmon

starter does just this by perfectly fusing together sweet and savoury. Their fresh, wholesome produce, as well as the modest portion sizes of the meals, make this a fantastic treat for those of us that have earnt our mouth-watering reward.

NAMA FOODS

110 TALBOT ROAD, NOTTING HILL, W11 1JR

OPEN

MON.	CLOSED
TUE-WED.	12:00AM - 10:00PM
THU.	12:00AM - 11:00PM
FRI-SAT.	9:00AM - 11:00PM
SUN.	9:00AM - 6:00PM

 NAMAFOODS.COM

LADBROKE GROVE

Don't be surprised to arrive at NAMA on a Saturday and find it bulging at the seams, but do wait for a table. Close to Portobello Market, but just far enough away to avoid those touristy crowds, NAMA focuses on the pure quality of its raw offerings. If you're passing by in a hurry, pick up NAMA's signature superfood latte (an infusion like no other containing lúcuma, coconut oil, plant milk, vanilla, maca, white carob and medicinal mushrooms), or one of their cold-pressed juices or smoothies. The raw menu replicates popular dishes in a clean, creative and flavoursome

manner. We recommend heading down for brunch, and ordering a 'build your own raw breakfast'. From cashew and coconut 'scrambled eggs' to artisan 'raw toast', it's a different and exciting way of doing things.

NOPI

21 - 22 WARWICK STREET, SOHO, W1B 5NE

OPEN

MON-FRI.	8:00AM - 10:30PM
SAT.	10:00AM - 10:30PM
SUN.	10:00AM - 4:00PM

OTTOLENGHI.CO.UK

OXFORD CIRCUS /
PICCADILLY CIRCUS

This upmarket Soho brasserie ties together intricate contemporary design nodding to bygone times in far-off places, with experimental vegetarian cooking that pelts straight ahead to the future. Designed by world-renowned architect Alex Meitlis, it's a treat for the eyes. Golden Spider Grecian pink marble tiles span the floor; brass lamps are replicas of one found in the flea market in Jaffa, Tel Aviv; and the ornate leaf light above reception is a signature of designer and artist Tommaso Barbi, who was prominent in the 60s and 70s. This carefully conceptualised environment showcases NOPI food and drinks, made with care and artistic flare; case in point, a Josephine King painting prominently mounted on the end wall is titled, 'I told him I was an artist. He said, "can you cook?"' Whilst the menu evolves with season, aubergine always takes pride of place (the Wi-Fi password is aubergine), and courgette and manouri fritters are a long time favourite. Here, even the cocktails are made with fresh fruit and vegetables; we suggest the Sumac Martini. With beautiful flowers, and video art flickering onto a wall, this is a forward-thinking, gorgeous environment in which to enjoy experimental yet wholesome cuisine.

OPEN

MON-FRI.   8:00AM - 8:00PM
SAT.   8:00AM - 7:00PM
SUN.   8:30AM - 6:00PM

 OTTOLENGHI.CO.UK

NOTTING HILL GATE /
LADBROKE GROVE

OTTOLENGHI

13 MOTCOMB STREET, BELGRAVIA, SW1X 8LB

Well-known for his culinary delights, Ottolenghi rarely disappoints. Colourful salads and slices of quiche are beautifully displayed to catch your attention through the large glassy window at the front. Most of the shop is taken up by the presentation of the food, though there is a communal round table at the back for anyone looking to eat in. The menu is ever-changing and there is a real dedication to detail in the touch of Middle Eastern and North African flavours and ingredients used. Ottolenghi hits the nail on the head when it comes to fresh, seasonal combinations. Whether you're tempted by the pea and mint fritters with lime and chive yogurt, or the beetroot and cumin mash with root vegetable crisps and crispy kale, the choice of what to choose brings back happy memories of that childhood pick n' mix. Natural and nutritious, Ottolenghi has worked hard to earn and maintain its fantastic reputation.

QUEENSWOOD

15 BATTERSEA SQUARE, BATTERSEA, SW11 3RA

OPEN

MON-SAT.	8:00AM - 11:00PM
SUN.	9:00AM - 6:00PM

 QUEENSWOODLDN.COM

CLAPHAM JUNCTION RAIL

A fantastic addition to Battersea Square, Queenswood is a wholesome and flavourful find that has an all-important yet underlying focus on healthier food. The cauli-steak or the heritage beetroot risotto will have you pining for more plant-based goodness, and the squash and carrot dumplings are simply to dine for. You can head here during the day or for dinner and dessert, there are menus to suit. Vegetarian-friendly with options like the Brunch Bowl: a tasty combination of lentils, avocado, pomegranate, seeds and egg, there are also creative vegan options, and certain dishes are easily altered upon request. The classic 'AVOCADO' is a brunchtime winner, served on sourdough toast with pomegranate, seeds, egg or feta - it's a handy hangover cure.

RABBIT

172 KING'S ROAD, CHELSEA, SW3 4UP

OPEN

MON.	6:00PM - 11:00PM
TUE-SAT.	12:00PM - 12:00AM
SUN.	12:00PM - 6:00PM

 RABBIT-RESTAURANT.COM

 SLOANE SQUARE

On a piece of corrugated steel sheeting, there - in bold, black letters - spells 'RABBIT' the simple yet catchy name of this quintessentially British restaurant. In prime location on the King's Road, here you'll find food that's fresh, tasty and served straight from farm to table. With barnlike décor to match, the food and surroundings create a countrified vibe that's a pleasant contrast to the usual 'London' look. Owned by the three Gladwin brothers, one is a farmer, one a chef and the other specialised in hospitality - all the essential ingredients to make a successful family restaurant! Serving classically British cuisine, the Rabbit menu focuses on seasonal and sustainable ingredients that, if not sourced from their own farm in Sussex, derived from splendid local sources across the UK.

RAWDUCK

197 RICHMOND ROAD, HACKNEY, E8 3NJ

OPEN

MON.	6:00AM - 10.30PM
TUE-SAT.	10:00AM - 10.30PM
SUN.	10:00AM - 9.30PM

🌐 RAWDUCKHACKNEY.CO.UK

🚆 LONDON FIELDS RAIL

The sister restaurant of Ducksoup in Soho, Raw Duck is similar in its focus on simple seasonal cooking. Everything on the menu is made in-house and from scratch. They offer a range of fermented drinks and foods which include kombuchas, drinking vinegars and kefirs, all believed to have a number of great benefits to your gut health. Found just a short walk from London Fields station, Raw Duck has a mellow buzz that fits in perfectly with this trendy Hackney neighbourhood. With long tables, as well as tall wooden stalls that look onto the kitchen, there are plenty of places to sit and enjoy the organic and biodynamic wine. Breakfast is served from 10am, lunch from noon and dinner from 6pm. We recommend coming here with family and friends to enjoy the sharing plates, but for large groups be sure to book ahead. If you're visiting Rawduck for weekend brunch, word on the street is that their homemade granola bowl is the best in the business!

REDEMPTION

6 CHEPSTOW ROAD, NOTTING HILL, W2 5BH

OPEN

MON.	CLOSED
TUE-FRI.	12:00PM - 11:00PM
SAT.	10:00AM - 11:00PM
SUN.	10:00AM - 5:00PM

🌐 REDEMPTIONBAR.CO.UK

⊖ NOTTING HILL GATE / ROYAL OAK

Having hosted events for Stella McCartney, Marc Cain and Hoxton Hotel to name but a few, it's no surprise that this Notting Hill restaurant is hot news. 'Spoil yourself without spoiling yourself,' their motto reads; and with sugar-free, wheat-free, vegan dishes and a completely non-alcoholic bar, you can believe it. Here, it's about caring for yourself, plants and animals in an exciting, creative dining environment. Creative Director and Executive Chef, Andrea Waters firmly believes that making the healthy choice is glamorous, sexy and cool. The restaurant serves daily Buddah Bowls (a new special every day), as well as a daytime and evening menu. Highlights include firecracker cauli for mains, and buckwheat and chia pancakes tossed in coconut oil and topped with banana, coconut yoghurt, caramelised pecans and maple syrup for dessert. Don't expect to see the same dishes on the menu week-in week-out, though; they constantly change and evolve based on seasonality and the creative head chef Waters. With a sleek black and water blue interior and marble tables that have tiny cacti atop, this is an excellent dining experience. Coupled with unique, inspired food, you certainly don't have to be vegan to catch on. We're all in need of a little Redemption, wouldn't you say?

SEA CONTAINERS

20 UPPER GROUND, BANKSIDE, SE1 9PD

OPEN

MON-FRI.   6:30AM - 11:00PM
SAT-SUN.   7:00AM - 11:00PM

🌐 SEACONTAINERSRESTAURANT.COM

⊖ BLACKFRIARS

Looking out onto the River Thames, Sea Containers boasts magnificent views of London and its breathtaking city skyline. Inspired by the history of transatlantic travel between the UK and the USA, the cuisine is an interesting blend of British and American with a Mediterranean twist. The themed interior of the restaurant submerges you into the world of travel and exploration; a wonderful backdrop to the seasonal, farm-to-table food on the menu. With three sections: 'From the Field', 'From the Sea' and 'From the Land' many of the plates are designed for sharing and the modest portion sizes make it hard to overindulge. With a mix of curved circular tables and long communal ones, the open kitchen at the back gives you a glimpse of your food being carefully prepared. The 'Raw Scallops' are a delicious choice, flavoured with ginger, shallots, sesame dressing and Arbequina olive oil, they simply melt in your mouth. As the sun slinks away and the afternoon turns to evening, candles and the dim lighting make this a truly romantic date spot. And love is essential to your health and wellbeing!

OPEN

MON.	CLOSED
TUE-WED.	8:00AM - 5:00PM
THU-SAT.	8:00AM - 11.30PM
SUN.	10:00AM - 5:00PM

 SNAPSANDRYE.COM

 LADBROKE GROVE / WESTBOURNE PARK

SNAPS + RYE

93 GOLDBORNE ROAD, LADBROKE GROVE, W10 5NL

Snaps + Rye, London's finest Danish café-restaurant, has a sense of tranquil goodness that's instantly palpable upon entrance; the polished white brick walls, potted jams and the smorgasbord of open sandwiches (Smørrebrød) decked with the freshest salmon strike a welcome tone. Try 'Sun over Golborne' for lunch, the restaurant's take on Danish classic 'Sol over Gudhjem'; a tantalising mix of smoked mackerel, egg yolk, rye, pickled beetroot, capers and radish. Alternatively, head over in the evening to get in on the £35 weekly changing set dinner menu (jazz it up with a bottle of wine; the Rhone Ventoux Rouge might not be Danish, but it's a goodie). Those in a rush are equally as well catered for, with fresh pastries, snacks and delicious specialty coffee also available.

SQUIRREL

11 HARRINGTON ROAD, SOUTH KENSINGTON, SW7 3ES

OPEN

MON-FRI.	7:00AM - 9:30PM
SAT.	8:00AM - 9:30PM
SUN.	9:00AM - 9:30PM

 WEARESQUIRREL.COM

SOUTH KENSINGTON

Just an acorn's throw away from South Kensington tube, Squirrel is London's latest treehouse of health. This spacious, wooded environment is as quirky as it is natural and delicious. In making healthy food fun and fun food healthy, Squirrel fills an interesting gap in the market. The freshly-made salads and warm grain bowls have names like 'Kale Yeah', 'Broc Chick', and 'Oh My Cobb' which tell you that this isn't just about food, it's about the outdoors, the adventure and the enjoyment of eating well. This is a great spot to bring the kids; it's fast food without the naughtiness. Every dish is made individually, with the ingredients laid out in the counter in front of you (carved from a fallen 21-foot long oak tree). The menu has all sorts of superfoods like dates, pecans, quinoa, cinnamon and almond butter as added extras. Whether you're going for the seasonal special or the classic 'Guac 'n' Roll', the staff are eager beavers to help you forage for your favourite combination.

WOKIT

3 STONEY STREET, SOUTHWARK, SE1 9AA

OPEN

MON-TUE.	11:30AM - 8:00PM
WED.	11:30AM - 8:30PM
THU.	11:30AM - 9:00PM
FRI.	11:00AM - 10:00PM
SAT.	11:00AM - 9:00PM
SUN.	CLOSED

 WOKIT.CO.UK

 LONDON BRIDGE

     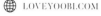

Looking on to the hustle and bustle of Borough Market, WOKIT make it their business to serve up a mean stir-fry. You pick your base of noodles or rice, then mix in a combination of vegetables & protein and watch them WOKIT up right there and then. If you prefer not to be the master of your own pot, their menu also has a 'combinations we love' section to speed up the process for anyone in a rush. With fresh vegetables arriving daily from their neighbours in Borough Market, WOKIT use local produce to

create a variety of delicious Asian flavours. The shop itself has only a few small tables, so you might have to wait if you were hoping to eat in. This place feels lovingly put together, not refined or polished, but hearty and wholesome.

YOOBI

38 LEXINGTON STREET, SOHO, W1F 0LL

OPEN

MON-SAT.	11:30AM - 9:00PM
SUN.	CLOSED

 LOVEYOOBI.COM

 PICCADILLY CIRCUS / OXFORD STREET

In the heart of Soho, Yoobi brings a fusion of Japanese food with added Brazilian flavours to London's creative crowd. Situated on Lexington street, this temakeria calls itself 'a playground for sushi' which, complimented by the colourful vibe and design of the restaurant, makes it a particularly novel eating experience. For those who are new to temaki, this is fresh sushi wrapped in a crispy seaweed cone - an original take on the old-school sandwich! Certainly not what you'd call a cheap find if you're hungry to try a range of their sushi, sashimi, soups or salads.

However, Yoobi does use their own rice blend, as well as sustainably sourced fish and locally sourced vegetables - so you do get what you pay for!

GUT HEALTH: OUR MICROBIAL UNIVERSE

BY **THE LONDON WELLNESS GUIDE**

WHAT DOES YOUR GUT TELL YOU?

There are tens of trillions of bacteria inside you right now, and far from being harmful, they are essential to keeping you alive. This is your microbiome - a thriving community of gut-dwelling bacteria that helps the body function. Our unique microbial identity influences our moods, immune system, emotions and even long-term health. In fact, much of how we feel is determined by chemical activity in the gut, which the brain then interprets as emotions - around 95% of your body's serotonin (linked to feelings of happiness) can be found in the gut, so we really do feel with our gut first! It's no wonder that scientists are calling the microbiome your second brain.

We're told to 'trust your gut', and for good reason. Perhaps instinctively, we always knew that there was far more going on in there than we had ever previously imagined.

A PLACE TO CALL HOME

We have around 1kg of bacteria inside our gut. It's a diverse community with different strains of microbes playing specific roles within the body. Some are merely passengers, whereas others are essential for good health. Our bacteria helps to digest food, educate the immune system, protect us from disease and even guide aspects of behaviour. The more diverse our microbiome, the better - studies show that less bacterial diversity has been linked to various stress disorders, and even autism. Diversity also leaves us better equipped to deal with attacks on the immune system, so we're less likely to catch that office lurgy. It's a delicate balance and one that we, as hosts, need to support in order to help our good bacteria to thrive.

GRUMPY GUTS?

An unhappy gut can cause a range of problems and make us miserable to boot. From gas, bloating and diarrhoea to the presence of depression, autoimmune and neuromuscular diseases - symptoms can range from merely uncomfortable, to chronic and debilitating. According to the NHS, around 40% of people have at least one digestive symptom at any one time, which can play havoc to our overall wellbeing.

MODERN WOES

It's no coincidence that gut complaints are plaguing the developed world with many aspects of modern diet and lifestyle being held accountable. Whether it's a diet high in refined carbs, sugars, artificial sweeteners and processed foods, the rise of antibiotic use, increased exposure to environmental toxins (such as pollution and cleaning agents) or high stress levels - these daily realities are thought to be decimating our microbiome, reducing the diversity in bacteria and jeopardizing the delicate balance.

A BUMPY START

The increase in caesarean births and decrease in breastfeeding in the West has also been pinpointed for blame. When a baby is born via the mother's birth canal, it is welcomed by a plethora of bacteria en route, which then forms the basis of its own microbiome. When breastfed, 1/3 of the mother's milk is made up of a unique form of carbohydrates (known as prebiotics) that specifically feed these good bacteria in the gut, further strengthening the baby's immune system. Our increased reliance on formula milk has left babies missing out on the essential, gut-boosting nutrients that breast milk contains. Keeping things natural where possible gives babies' immune systems a vital helping hand, reducing their risk of allergies and autoimmune diseases later on, and giving them the best possible start.

MAINTAINING ORDER

As hosts to these tens of trillions of bacteria, it is up to us to eat and live in a way that will support a healthy balance in our microbial universe. Luckily, there are all sorts of ways in which we can do this, from what we nourish our bodies with to how we manage stress (the less of it, the better!). The more diverse and nutrient-dense our diet, the healthier we will be on a microbial level, keeping both our mind and gut happy.

PROBIOTIC PROTECTION

The term 'probiotic' has been catapulted into public awareness by 'friendly, bacteria-promoting' dairy products throughout the past decade. 'Probiotics' are good bacteria, found in fermented foods like natural yoghurt, which help tip the microbial balance in our favour. Sources of probiotics include quark, kefir, live sauerkraut, miso, kimchi and non-pasteurized pickled vegetables. Although, one thing to beware: many probiotic products that can be bought in supermarkets are packed with hidden, refined sugars, which may undermine any health-giving benefits that they claim to provide, so check the label to be on the safe side!

PREBIOTIC GOODNESS

Another way to maintain a good gut balance is by eating more 'prebiotic' foods. Prebiotics are a form of carbohydrate that feed the beneficial bacteria. And you don't need to trek to your nearest health food shop to find them - oats, fennel, apples, pak choi, leeks, cold potatoes, bananas, berries, legumes, onions, garlic and asparagus are all fantastic sources. So, an oat-based breakfast topped with live, natural yoghurt, banana and berries will give your gut a robust start to the day and

leave you feeling more energised too.

BACK TO BASICS

Foods containing antioxidants also feed the goodies in your gut. Reap the rewards with seeds, nuts, extra virgin olive oil, coffee, dark chocolate and even red wine (within reason). As a general rule, the more natural and 'whole' your food is - i.e. a diet which is closer to that of our hunter-gatherer ancestors - the greater your microbial diversity and the fitter you will feel. So stocking up on whole grains and fibrous vegetables will get you well on your way to rediscovering your inner balance, in both mind and gut.

GETTING TO THE BOTTOM OF IT

We're still in the infant stages of discovering the immense power of this hidden, internal world and understanding the full implications on our health and wellbeing. The evidence so far, however, is remarkable. Scientists have discovered that transferring the microbiome from one living thing to another (via a faecal transplant) can radically alter mood, behaviour, and even body weight. This could open up exciting possibilities for various new treatments. We're entering an era where human faecal transplants may become mainstream.

If the gut is our second brain then we need to take good care of it. It might be as simple as ditching the extreme-clean habit (antibacterial products kill both good and bad bacteria), eating more pre and probiotic foods, and embracing the mud on those farm-bought potatoes - all in the name of supporting that thriving inner community. The more we discover, the more exciting it is for the future of both our physical and mental wellness. So look after your gut, and it will look after you.

OPEN

MON–SAT.	7:00AM - 10:00PM
SUN.	8:00AM - 8:00PM

 CPRESSJUICE.COM

 SOUTH KENSINGTON /
GLOUCESTER ROAD

CPRESS

285 FULHAM ROAD, CHELSEA, SW10 9PZ

We might as well have sauntered straight off Sunset Boulevard in chichi LA; this ultramodern juice bar will remind you of those found on the trendy Californian coast. Situated on the Fulham Road, CPRESS is often filled with a mixture of regular juicers awaiting their daily fix as well as the new and curious passer-by. With fun names like Flamingo and Coco Loco, the cold-pressed juice selection makes drinking your greens all the easier. Though if you'd rather smoothies, coffees or colourful superfood salad bowls, they can also be found on the mainly raw, gluten-free, vegan, refined sugar-free and dairy-free menu. With white marble tables and magazines neatly placed in racks, there is something particularly photo-friendly about the stylish simplicity of this place. The custom geometric wood wall, sleek and aesthetically pleasing to the eye, reflects the simple yet delicious (and organic) combinations of fruits and flavours in the juices. No doubt this it is where the fitness fanatics hang out and share their tips.

EAST LONDON JUICE CO.

100 SHOREDITCH HIGH STREET, SHOREDITCH, E16 JQ

OPEN

MON-SUN.   7:00AM - 9:00PM

EASTLONDONJUICE.COM

SHOREDITCH HIGH STREET

Art, nutrition and responsibility come together at 100 Shoreditch High Street, in a small takeaway booth poking out from Ace Hotel. Unlike other such booths, East London Juice Co. is about anything but fast food. Clear attention to detail is obvious; as if it were an apothecary, hundreds of bottles and containers line rows of shelves, potted plants hang from the ceiling and curious natural stones are displayed in jars. These bottles and seed containers - bearing almost mythical ingredients, like marine phytoplankton and spirulina - come together to make Hot Elixirs, smoothies, mylks and other potion-like drinks. The ingredients here focus on nurturing the body, delivering all sorts of goodness that is unheard of elsewhere (see their online Field Notes, detailing some of these ingredients, and what each claims to do). These are makers - not just distributors - activating, fermenting and distilling organic, fairly-traded or wild-harvested ingredients to craft botanic and medicinal combinations. Whilst interesting, responsible methods are a certain draw, the food matches up in flavour. Don't leave without a waffle bowl; made of more ingredients than you can imagine, they are packed full of flavour - from a sprinkling of bee pollen to a smattering of maple sap. The acai bowl, is also a must try.

GRILL MARKET

293 FULHAM ROAD, CHELSEA, SW10 9PZ

OPEN

MON-FRI.   7:30AM - 8:30PM

SAT-SUN.   9:00AM - 5:00PM

🌐 GRILLMARKET.CO.UK

🚇 SOUTH KENSINGTON

With beetroot, turmeric and matcha lattes on their menu, the variety of healthy options at Grill Market makes it an easy addition to this London Wellness Guide. Conveniently located below the LOMAX gym on the Fulham Road, this great little café serves some truly delicious smoothies and juices. The Bees Knees Protein Shake is an absolute must: blueberries, banana, honey and chia seeds - you get that sweet taste with none of the naughtiness! With casual wooden tables and a dog-friendly attitude, Grill Market exudes a certain charm that lures you in to stay longer than expected. Great for pre-fuel or re-fuel if you're taking a fitness class, it's a comfortable spot to catch up with friends or perhaps your fitness blog? Vegetarians close your eyes as the fresh fish, meat and poultry look particularly good, though the deli style salads are freshly tossed and ready to be tucked in to. Thank goodness all the baked treats are refined sugar-free - a perfect excuse to indulge... you've earnt it.

JOE & THE JUICE

65 - 67 BROADWICK STREET, SOHO, W1F 9QY

OPEN

MON-FRI.   8:00AM - 8:00PM

SAT-SUN.   10:00AM - 8:00PM

 JOEJUICE.COM

OXFORD CIRCUS /
PICCADILLY CIRCUS

Though Joe & The Juice might at first sound like a 90s band that never made the big time, it is in fact an uber-trendy addition to London's evolving café scene. This Danish brand was founded in 2002 by Kaspar Basse and now has stores not just across London but across the world. Bringing juice to the masses at rapid pace, the signature style, culture and vibe in these bars is fun and often hard to find. With an emphasis on fresh music, as well as fresh food and service; these stores make juices and smoothies to order - they also make it look cool. The exotic ingredients range from bananas to pineapples, carrots, mint, ginger and acai to name just a few. They also serve a great 'cup of Joe' - the American slang for coffee - which is where the brand name derived. The comfy couches here make this a desirable place to put your feet up and chill. Nothing better than fresh juice for a fresh perspective.

OPEN

MON–SAT.	8:00AM – 7:00PM
SUN.	9:00AM – 7:00PM

 JUICEBABY.CO.UK

FULHAM BROADWAY

JUICEBABY

398 KING'S ROAD, CHELSEA, SW10 0LJ

It's all in the name with Juicebaby - young, fun and freshly cold-pressed. This café, situated on the King's Road just a few doors down from TriYoga Chelsea, is a great spot for meet ups and feet ups. As you enter, the large communal table to your left has sofa style seating which can lure you in for hours on end. The quirky names of the juices, meals, snacks and desserts disguises the fact they are all 100% vegan and completely plant-based. There is a dizzying selection of nectarous treats; whether it's the Peanut Butter Florentines, the Tart Lemon Mousse or the Chocolate Krispies, Juicebaby makes the point that eating natural does not need to be boring. Their philosophy is 'little by little', because the little choices make a big difference. So then the question is: 'What to get?' - the Mean Green, the Green Glow, or the Green Easy juice?

LITTLE H

267 NEW KING'S ROAD, FULHAM, SW6 4RB

OPEN

MON-FRI.   7:30AM - 5:30PM
SAT-SUN.   9:00AM - 5:30PM

 LITTLEHLONDON.COM

PARSONS GREEN

Just across the road from Hally's, Little H, its deli-cum-café-cum-juice bar little sibling, has its very own stylish space. Founded by husband and wife team, Amanda Halliday and Philip Beatty, they've made it difficult to pass by this bright yellow shop and its modern glass-fronted window without being tempted to pop in. Adopting the same farm-to-table approach as Hally's, as well as delicious vegan, wheat, dairy and sugar-free options, Little H is different in that it mainly caters for customers looking to get their spiralized goodness to go. Having said that, there are a few high tables and a bar at the front for those looking to make the most of this (naturally) sweet little eatery. The extensive juice and smoothie menu is the real jewel here, allowing you to create your own concoction should you feel like something bespoke. So, with lucuma, maca, spirulina, wheatgrass, hemp protein, cashews and bee pollen just a few of the ingredients that can be added to your drink, what magic concoction will you conjure up?

PRESS

6 DENMAN STREET, SOHO, W1D 7HD

OPEN

MON-FRI. 8:00AM - 5:30PM

SAT-SUN. CLOSED

 PRESS-LONDON.COM

 PICCADILLY CIRCUS

For those in the know, PRESS really is the watering hole of the 'urban healthies'. Its flagship store can be found on Denman Street, conveniently located just a two-minute walk from Piccadilly Circus. Its ultra-slick design showcases an enviable array of cold-pressed juices and superfood soups. The combination of vibrant colours behind the glass refrigerators seems to be what healthy looks like bottled-up. The Orchard 1 with its blend of strawberry, apple, lemon and mint, tastes sweet like summer feels. By comparison, the Greenhouse 5 and its spicy jalapeno kick is a dare-devil option for the chilli-chasers out there. Serving more than just juice, PRESS sells a variety of nut-milk shakes, health tonic shots, superfood salads and soups. The avocado toast drizzled with a choice of argan, truffle or olive oil and sprinkled with chilli flakes is Soho's best kept secret. That, and their Cacao Leche, a dairy-free chocolate indulgence. If you've fallen off the health food wagon and you're looking for a way to get back on track, we suggest coming here to PRESS reset.

RAW PRESS

32 DOVER STREET, MAYFAIR, W1S 4NE

OPEN

MON-THU.	8:00AM - 6:00PM
FRI.	8:00AM - 5:00PM
SAT-SUN.	CLOSED

 RAWPRESS.CO

GREEN PARK

If you're seeking out London's underground juice bars, then Raw Press, beneath Wolfe & Badger on Dover Street, is a fantastic find. Well-hidden, like many of Mayfair's treasure coves, Raw Press specializes in raw, organic, cold-pressed juice. They have combinations ranging from beetroot, carrot, apple, fennel and horseradish, to orange, grapefruit, apple, lemon, lime and thyme - all aboard the superfood express. Though if you're not one for a liquid lunch, they also serve a variety of freshly-made salads, daily soup and sweet snacks, as well as sweet strawberry acai, chia pots and granola bowls for breakfast. With one large communal table, this juice bar makes for a cosy co-working space, one that gets particularly packed at lunchtime when regulars pop by to pick up their nutritious nibbles. All sorts of conversations pop up over the shared toasters set out along the table. The Pip n' Nut Nutbutters make it easy to spread the love. For anyone looking for a coffee alternative, this is your happy place - with turmeric, matcha and chai on the menu, there's a-latte choice!

ROOTS JUICERY

1 CHARLOTTE PLACE, FITZROVIA, W1T 1SA

OPEN

MON-FRI.	8:00AM - 6:00PM
SAT.	10:00AM - 5:00PM
SUN.	CLOSED

🌐 ROOTSJUICERY.CO.UK

Ⓔ GOODGE STREET / TOTTENHAM COURT ROAD

Roots Juicery is one of Fitzrovia's finest juice bars. The wooden floor boards, tables and benches give this shop a natural air of bohemian chic. The organic, cold-pressed juices come in dainty glass bottles and the outdoor seating makes this a charming summertime spot. Just as the shop steers clear of being overly stylized or clinical, so too does the food. The homemade banana bread, key lime pie and quinoa cookies are worth telling your friends about - or NOT telling your friends about so you can keep them to yourself... The glass

cabinet at the front displays the freshly made goodies that are naturally sweet and perfect for an afternoon pick-me-up. They also serve nut mylks, superfood smoothies and porridge pots to keep you content.

SHOT

23 BRIDE LANE, TEMPLE, EC4Y 8DT

OPEN

MON-FRI.	7:00AM - 3:00PM | 6:00PM - 10:00PM
SAT-SUN.	CLOSED

🌐 SHOT.LONDON

Ⓔ BLACKFRIARS / ST PAUL'S

A subtle turning off Fleet Street will lead you straight to SHOT. This delicious juice bar serves wheatgrass instead of whiskey - exactly what stressed-out city workers need! Serving only organic food and drink, the cold-pressed juices here are completely chemical-free. Using zero additives, preservatives, flavourings or colourings, SHOT have built their brand around healthy living and healthy eating. Everything is made fresh on-site, so personalised preferences can be considered. They cater for gluten free, dairy free, vegetarians and vegans alike, as well as those who simply want

a break from sugary, processed foods. The large, multi-coloured neon SHOT sign over the fridge reflects the colourful and feel-good flavours of the salads, sandwiches and superfood smoothies served up in front of you.

SUPERNATURAL

UNIT 4, CANARY WHARF UNDERGROUND STATION, CANARY WHARF, E14 4HJ

OPEN

MON-SUN. 6:00AM - 9:00PM

 SPRNTRL.CO.UK

 CANARY WHARF

As delicious as they are colourful, the Supernatural juices and smoothies are an early morning must. Their flagship Canary Wharf store is located in the Underground station next to the Jubilee Line ticket barrier. This store has what every busy, burnt-out banker needs - a Mango Passion Pina Colada with mango, pineapple, passionfruit and coconut milk, it's the ticket to a better day. Putting health on the menu, Supernatural also offers Positivitea, Bullet Proof Coffee and Vegan Hot Chocolate, in addition to their staple fresh juices, smoothies and shakes. Crafted by mixologists and nutritionists they fuse flavour with wellbeing and offer an obvious alternative to fizzy drinks at lunchtime. Expanding quickly across London, it's no surprise that these stores have gone down as well as the Jamaica Juice they serve. With nowhere to sit, this Canary Wharf Supernatural is grab n' go, which tends to suit the smartly dressed professionals looking for their gourmet porridge or cacao coconut chia pudding to eat at their desk. Is it a plane? Is it a bird? No. It's Supernatural.

BETTER WAYS OF EATING FOR LIFE

BY **DALE PINNOCK,** SANO SCHOOL OF CULINARY MEDICINE

Just made the choice to eat healthier? Getting confused with conflicting messages? I feel your pain. It's a muddy minefield at times, but in the general scheme of things, it needn't be. I believe that for most people, the 3 simple actions below can make a world of difference to overall long term health. This isn't calorie counting or weight loss, it's simply better ways of eating to support good health for life.

GET YOUR FATS STRAIGHT

Fat has always had a bad reputation when it comes to diet and health. These views are beginning to change, however the types of fats that we are consuming need serious attention. Far too many of us are consuming high amounts of processed plant derived oils, such as sunflower oil, soy oil, and regular vegetable oils. Movement away from oils like butter and lard in favour of margarine, and the consumption of more processed food and ready meals has meant that our intake has become rather high. For generations we were told to move away from saturated fat laden butter and lard, and choose the 'heart healthy' vegetable oils instead. This caused more damage than anyone could have expected. Processed vegetable oils are high in omega 6, a fatty acid that we need in very small amounts. Exceeding that amount, can cause omega 6 to convert into compounds that activate and exacerbate inflammation.

Inflammation is an essential response in the body, but when it goes into overdrive it can be the root cause of many diseases as well as a powerful exacerbating factor. Increased omega 6, means increased pro-inflammatory compounds, resulting in more inflammation, leading to increased disease risk. One of the biggest killers linked to inflammation is heart disease. Heart disease is essentially an inflammatory condition. Minute inflammatory events can damage the endothelium - the skin that lines the inside of our blood vessels. It is this initial inflammatory injury that then sets in motion the series of events that eventually lead to plaque formation in the arteries. Cutting these oils right down and increasing our intake of omega 3 fatty acids can drastically reduce inflammation in the body.

Omega 3 fatty acids are like the angelic twin of the omega 6, vastly important in human health, but often something we are deficient in. There are a few different types of omega 3. Two of them, EPA and DHA found in foods like oily fish and grass fed meats, can produce powerful anti-inflammatory compounds.

GET CARB SMART

The type of carbohydrates that we consume can have a huge impact on our health. Now this isn't advice to suddenly adopt a low carb diet or avoid them completely, rather to be conscious of the types you choose. The best thing to do is to ditch white refined versions (white bread, white rice, white pasta etc.) and choose brown multigrain varieties instead. The refined white versions are digested very quickly and release their energy straight away. This causes our blood sugar to rise rapidly, sending it higher than is safe. In response to this we release the hormone insulin. This tells our cells that there is excess sugar available, and allows them to take up this sugar and utilise it for energy. Now, in small assaults, this scenario is no major issue, however eating lots of these refined carbohydrates overburdens our system. This leads to our body pumping out insulin consistently and our insulin receptors soon start to 'ignore' insulin. We become insulin resistant, making it harder to clear blood sugar. Initially the body tries to deal with the problem by secreting more insulin, which works for a while. Eventually though insulin receptors really dig their heels in and resist insulin's message. At this point we are teetering on the edge of type 2 diabetes. As insulin's signal isn't getting through, blood sugar remains dangerously high, which eventually causes toxicity to many tissues, including the beta cells in the pancreas, leading to type 2 diabetes.

It doesn't end there though, as these foods can affect the health of our hearts too. In the context of heart disease, if our blood sugar gets too high for too long, our cells soon get full, and the body finds other ways to get blood sugar levels down. The main way that it does this is send excess sugar to the liver, where it is turned into a kind of fat called Triacylglycerol, that can be stored in fat tissue for a rainy day. This fat is transported to fat tissue via the bloodstream. When it moves through our circulatory system, it is very susceptible to oxidation and can trigger inflammatory damage to the endothelium, the inner lining of the blood vessels, triggering a cascade of responses that attempt to repair the damage. This repair response leads to the plaques characteristic of heart disease.

GET FRESH

The final part of the picture when it comes to simple strategies for everyday health, is to look for as many opportunities as possible to get fresh plant foods into your diet. This could be as simple as topping your morning porridge with berries, occasional fresh fruit between meals, and having a big varied side salad with your lunch and dinner, ensuring you have a variety of colours on your plate etc. Nothing complex, but this can have a big impact. Why? It's all about the micronutrients. Nutrients sit in two categories - macronutrients and micronutrients. The macronutrients are the proteins, fats and carbohydrates, and the micronutrients are the vitamins, minerals, and trace elements. This latter group are so vital, they could never be overplayed. Think of them as biochemical facilitators. They either directly make chemical reactions in the body happen, or make the things that make chemical reactions happen. They are so vital to our everyday physical functioning, that even small drops in them can have profound consequences. Surprise surprise they aren't found in processed dead foods. Get fresh folks!

sanoschoolofculinarymedicine.com

HEALTH FOOD STORES

APPLEJACKS
28 THE MALL, STRATFORD,
E15 1XD
OPEN
MON-WED.	9:00AM - 6:00PM
THU-FRI.	8:00AM - 7:00PM
SAT.	9:00AM - 6:00PM
SUN.	10:30AM - 4:00PM

⊖ STRATFORD

AS NATURE INTENDED
THE EXCHANGE BUILDING,
132 COMMERCIAL STREET,
SHOREDITCH, E1 6NG
OPEN
MON-FRI.	9:00AM - 8:00PM
SAT-SUN.	10:00AM - 8:00PM

⊖ SHOREDITCH HIGH STREET

BUMBLEBEE NATURAL FOODS
33 BRECKNOCK ROAD,
HOLLOWAY, E1 6NG
OPEN
MON-SAT.	9:00AM - 6:30PM
SUN.	CLOSED

⊖ KENTISH TOWN

EARTH NATURAL FOODS
200 - 202 KENTISH TOWN
ROAD, BELSIZE PARK, NW5 2AE
OPEN
MON-SAT.	8:30AM - 7:00PM
SUN.	CLOSED

⊖ KENTISH TOWN

G BALDWIN AND CO
171 - 173 WALWORTH ROAD,
ELEPHANT AND CASTLE,
SE17 1RW
OPEN
MON-SAT.	9:00AM - 6:00PM
SUN.	CLOSED

⇌ ELEPHANT AND CASTLE

GREENBAY
BRAMBER COURT, 228 NORTH
END ROAD, FULHAM, W14 9NU
OPEN
MON-SAT.	10:00AM - 8:00PM
SUN.	10:00AM - 6:00PM

⊖ WEST BROMPTON

HARA
231 FINCHLEY ROAD,
HAMPSTEAD, NW3 6LS
OPEN
MON-FRI.	9:30AM - 6:30PM
SAT.	9:30AM - 5:30PM
SUN.	CLOSED

⊖ FINCHLEY ROAD

HARVEST E8
130 - 132 KINGSLAND HIGH
STREET, DALSTON, E8 2NS
OPEN
MON-SAT.	7:00AM - 10:00PM
SUN.	9:00AM - 9:00PM

⊖ DALSTON KINGSLAND

HEALTHMATTERS
47 LORDSHIP LANE, EAST
DULWICH, SE22 8EP
OPEN
MON-SAT.	9:00AM - 5.45PM
SUN.	10:30AM - 4:30PM

⇌ EAST DULWICH

HOLLAND & BARRETT FLAGSHIP
526 OXFORD STREET,
MARYLEBONE, W1C 1LW
OPEN
MON-FRI.	9:00AM - 8:00PM
SAT.	10:00AM - 8:00PM
SUN.	11:30AM - 6:00PM

⊖ MARBLE ARCH

**MOTHER EARTH CAFÉ
AND SHOP**
101 - 103 NEWINGTON GREEN RD,
SHACKLEWELL, N1 4QY
OPEN
MON-FRI.	8:30AM - 8:00PM
SAT.	9:00AM - 8:00PM
SUN.	10:00AM - 7:00PM

⊖ CANONBURY

OLIVERS WHOLEFOOD STORE
5 STATION APPROACH, KEW
GARDENS, TW9 3QB
OPEN
MON-SAT.	9:00AM - 8:30PM
SUN.	10:00AM - 8:30PM

⊖ KEW GARDENS

PLANET ORGANIC
22 TORRINGTON PLACE,
BLOOMSBURY, WC1E 7HJ
OPEN
MON-FRI.	7:30AM - 9:00PM
SAT.	8:00AM - 8:00PM
SUN.	12:00AM - 6:00PM

⊖ GOODGE STREET

REVITAL
22 WIGMORE STREET,
MARYLEBONE, W1U 2RG
OPEN
MON-FRI.	9:00AM - 7:00PM
SAT.	10:00AM - 6:00PM
SUN.	11:00AM - 4:00PM

⊖ BOND STREET

WHOLEFOODS
63 - 97 KENSINGTON HIGH
STREET, KENSINGTON, W8 5SE
OPEN
MON-SAT.	8:00AM - 10:00PM
SUN.	12:00PM - 6:00PM

⊖ HIGH STREET KENSINGTON

ABOKADO

UNIT 3, 104 - 122 CITY ROAD, IMPERIAL HALL, SHOREDITCH, EC1V 2NR

OPEN

MON-FRI.   6:30AM - 9:00PM

SAT-SUN.   CLOSED

🌐 ABOKADO.COM

🚇 OLD STREET

Inspired by the variety of healthy options and eateries in Sydney during a round the world trip in 2002, Mark and Lindsay Lilly came back to the UK with a plan to bring a good value sushi, juice and noodle bars to a then soggy London sandwich scene. And that's exactly what they've done given that they now have around 30 shops spread over the city of London and the West End. Particularly if you're trying to keep track of what and how much you eat, all the products in store show exactly what goes in to the recipes, the number of calories, total fat and saturated fat. Their 'feel great food' strikes

an important balance between healthy and wholesome, without being overly calorific. With sushi boxes, hot pots, bagels, wraps and sushi shwraps, as well as fresh juices and cheeky sweet treats; Abokado is helping Londoner's change up their lunchbox one gyoza at a time!

CHOP'D

52 CURZON STREET, MAYFAIR, W1J 7UP

OPEN

MON-FRI.   7:00AM - 3:00PM

SAT-SUN.   CLOSED

🌐 CHOPD.CO.UK

🚇 GREEN PARK

With apples sourced from Kent, chickens from Essex, and tofu from Brick Lane, this customised saladerie is all about keeping it local. By extension, every ingredient is under scrutiny from the co-owners, Eddie Holmes and Allan Cook. Not convinced? Their asparagus - strictly served only when in season - comes from the same farm that supplied the royal wedding. Here, it's simple; either order in the shop, or use the online click and collect service, ideal for those in a rush. There is a pre-designed menu of house salads, as well as stews and snacks. But we suggest taking the reins and

really making it yours. Build your own salad, start with a base, add some house and deli items, then garnish, dress and Voilà. They also do corporate deliveries for offices that want to serve salad al desko.

CRUSSH

14 BROADWICK STREET, SOHO, W1F 8HR

OPEN

MON-FRI. 7:30AM - 5:00PM

SAT-SUN. CLOSED

 CRUSSH.COM

 OXFORD CIRCUS / TOTTENHAM COURT ROAD

Crussh was born out of a James Learmond's idea to open a juice bar back in 1998 and now you'll notice his stores popping up all over London. Serving raw juice, smoothies and fit food, he's giving busy Londoners their daily dose of grab n' go goodness. Keeping up with the latest trends in the field of superfoods, the freshly packaged options are clearly marked to let you know what's dairy-free, gluten-free, low-fat, organic, vegan, vegetarian or contains nuts - there's something to suit even

the fussiest among us. The hot food changes daily, though if the chicken, kale, ginger & ginseng soup is on the menu, it's always a feel-good favourite!

ITSU

UNIT 1, 30 SPITAL SQUARE, SPITALFIELDS, E1 6DX

OPEN

MON-FRI. 8:00AM - 8:00PM

SAT-SUN. 11:00AM - 7:00PM

 ITSU.COM

 LIVERPOOL STREET

Co-founded by Julian Metcalfe, the same man who has brought us Pret A Manger, itsu is fast-becoming one of London's best known healthy high street options. Using the slogan 'eat beautiful', the packaging of the food and design of the shops reflect this idea that what you eat determines how you look and how you feel, both inside and out. A pioneering attitude toward eating well and the needs of the consumer, itsu uses flavours from the Far East to create on the go meals that are low in calories and saturated fat, but remain nutritious and flavoursome. With a range

of noodle soups, brown rice potsus, packed low carb salads, freshly-made sushi and sashimi or even real fruit smoothies, the menu adapts slightly for the changing seasons. Half an hour before closing each store holds an itsu sale - all sushi and salad boxes for half price.

LEON

THE BLUE FIN BUILDING, 7 CANVEY STREET, SOUTHWARK, SE1 9AN

OPEN

MON-THU.	7:00AM - 9:00PM
FRI.	7:00AM - 10:00PM
SAT.	8:00AM - 10:00PM
SUN.	9:00AM - 8:00PM

 LEONRESTAURANTS.CO.UK

SOUTHWARK /
LONDON BRIDGE

When you're handed your brown paper bag at LEON, did you know that the simple packaging is based on those traditionally used by fruit pickers? This analogy purposefully reflects the simplicity of the ingredients that LEON serve. Bringing fast, Mediterranean freshness to the masses, LEON has been on a mission to make 'fast food that makes you feel good' mainstream since opening its first Carnaby Street store in 2004. Each store is adorned with photos from the co-founders' family albums to give it a homely, relatable vibe. No two branches are identical and though the branding is instantly recognizable, each store comes with its own character and charm. Serving Fairtrade and organic coffee, as well a combination of recipes that cater for vegetarians, nut allergies, gluten and dairy intolerances and people on a low carb diet, LEON work hard to ensure they have both happy customers and happy staff. Stop by in the morning for 'The Ruby Berry Porridge', noon for the original 'Super Salad' and dinner for their 'Thai Green Chicken Curry Hot Box'... easy peasy LEON squeezy.

OPEN

MON-THU.   7:30AM - 5:00PM
FRI.   7:30AM - 4:00PM
SAT-SUN.   CLOSED

🌐 POD.CO.UK

☉ TOTTENHAM COURT ROAD

POD

CENTRAL SAINT GILES PIAZZA, SEVEN DIALS, WC2H 8LQ

Inspired by fast but fresh food, the first Pod was opened in 2005. Now with 24 shops, the eatery is ideal for foodies who want to treat themselves to flavoursome meals that are still good for the body. With globally inspired and trendy recipes, the menu certainly isn't boring; peanut butter power porridge is a hot favourite for breakfast, as is shaksuka (eggs poached in tomato sauce with chillies, onions and spices). Singapore chicken laska soup makes for a delicious and nutritious lunch, and the immune boost blitz smoothie is perfect for stashing up on antioxidants. Pod tries to source local, seasonal food that, in turn, supports Britain's micro economies, adding 70 new lunch dishes in just one year. Traceable from field to fork, the kale comes with Red Tractor accreditation, the chicken is British free range, and they use Rain Forest Alliance coffee beans. With biofa natural paint (raw and renewable) and floor tiles made of 40% recycled material, even the shops are constructed as sustainably as possible.

PURE

85 GRACECHURCH STREET, THE CITY, EC3V 0AA

OPEN

MON-FRI.   7:00AM - 8:00PM

SAT-SUN.   CLOSED

 PURE.CO.UK

MONUMENT

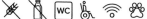

'Made for you' is the slogan of this popular London eatery, which aims to serve you made-to-order food within one minute of ordering. With fresh from the oven pastries and nourishing breakfasts available every morning, as well as freshly blended and bottled smoothies, Pure focuses on preserving the goodness of natural ingredients. To kick start your day in a tasty way, we recommend Super Eggs; served with your choice of toppings from sautéed mushrooms, to avocado or smoked salmon, for breakfast. The manuka honey blend organic porridge is also a nutritious and sweet way to get going. Pure's fast kitchen is a bonus for busy Londoners. There is something for everyone - from toasties to freshly dressed salads and hot boxes (the Thai Red Chicken is a favourite). If you have an office meeting, Pure will bike over a selection of food to accommodate the needs of your colleagues. What's more, they will swing by once you're done to collect and recycle the wooden trays that were delivered earlier. With the additional bonus of coffee ground to order, Pure offers rapid service, as well as food that's tasty and environmentally responsible.

TOSSED

4 BRUNSWICK SQUARE, BLOOMSBURY, WC1N 1BS

OPEN

MON-FRI.	7:00AM - 9:00PM
SAT.	8:30AM - 9:00PM
SUN.	9:00AM - 6:00PM

 TOSSEDUK.COM

 RUSSELL SQUARE

Slicker than slick, Tossed are helping to build the future of high-quality, healthy fast food. Their colour scheme is bright and jazzy which puts a fun twist on people's prejudice of 'boring old vegetables'. Since founding Tossed in 2005, Vincent McKevitt has been working tirelessly to make eating healthy both easy and accessible. The focus here is on good carbs, lean protein and getting in your 5 a day. The store in Russell Square lets customers order on their self-service iPads to allow people to order, eat and get on with the day. This quick and tasty salad bar concept is moving healthy to the masses, revolutionising the options for our time-poor grab n' go workers, what's not to love?

VEGGIE PRET

35 BROADWICK STREET, SOHO, W1F 0DH

OPEN

MON-FRI.	6:30AM - 9:00PM
SAT.	8:00AM - 8:00PM
SUN.	9:30AM - 7:00PM

 PRET.CO.UK

 OXFORD CIRCUS

Recognisable for its bright green entrance banner, Veggie Pret was initially another Soho pop-up destined to move on after one month. But in September 2016, it opened its doors as a permanent fixture for the first time, having proved remarkably popular with surrounding office workers and tourists alike. Packed out at breakfast and lunch time, the green space is full of plant-based treats, whilst still serving vegetarian Pret classics, like chocolate croissants and health shots. Veggie Pret's aim is to encourage meat eaters to try vegetarian and vegan produce

by making it look irresistibly good. Naturally, this plant-based fare is all freshly made in their on-site kitchen. The smoothies, which you pick up from the fridge for the staff to blend up, are delicious ways to get your daily dose of protein, nutrients and antioxidants.

VITAL INGREDIENT

1 GRESHAM STREET, BARBICAN, EC2V 7BX

OPEN

MON-FRI.   7:00AM - 4:30PM

SAT-SUN.   CLOSED

 VITALINGREDIENT.CO.UK

ST PAUL'S

Alex Heynes opened Vital Ingredient in 2001 to provide London with a new food concept - one that he himself was desperately searching for. Working in The City in the 90s, he was frustrated with the limited number of options for lunch besides the pre-made sandwiches. It was in New York where he caught the first glimpse of his future: a freshly tossed salad bar, where customers could choose exactly what they wanted. Inspired by Alex's farming background, Vital Ingredient, is based on the importance of quality, fresh ingredients that Londoners can get a hold of easily. One of a small chain across London, the St Pauls store offers up a selection of signature, legend and guest salads. We suggest going solo and choosing your own base, ingredients and dressing, to fix up a salad that works perfectly for you. Whilst salad helms the menu, the breakfast options are hard to resist. You can 'create your own' porridge, egg dish, protein pancakes, breakfast bowls or toasts. With a hot food menu to boot - featuring soups, jacket potatoes and street food that change weekly - Vital Ingredient is a fresh, fast and bespoke answer for hungry Londoners.

ONLINE DELIVERIES + SUBSCRIPTIONS

ABEL & COLE

Abel & Cole delivers boxes of fresh and organic fruit & veg, meat and fish, straight to your door. Personalise your box with produce that's in season. You can also order fantastic organic staples like bread, eggs and milk.

 ABELANDCOLE.CO.UK

THE DETOX KITCHEN

Chefs at The Detox Kitchen will make you breakfast, lunch, dinner, pressed juice and snacks using fresh, seasonal ingredients. Free from wheat, dairy and refined sugar, Detox Kitchen deliver your day's meals to your door. Healthy eating made easier.

 DETOXKITCHEN.CO.UK

FRESH FITNESS FOOD

Fresh Fitness Food is a premium meal delivery service offering fresh, quality food that is customised to your exact needs. The meals are assembled by their nutrition team, prepared by expert chefs and delivered daily to your home or work.

 FRESHFITNESSFOOD.COM

LOMAX FITFOOD

A unique collaboration between Lomax and Grill Market, FitFood makes it that much easier to stick to your nutrition plan. With thoughtfully designed, constantly changing menus, there are plenty of FitFood meals to keep you inspired.

 LOMAXPT.COM/
NUTRITION-2/FIT-FOOD

MINDFUL CHEF

Choose the recipes and Mindful Chef will source and deliver the exact ingredients needed for you to cook it up. These 100% gluten-free, easy to follow recipes take the stress out of meal planning. Make it easy, make it Mindful.

 MINDFULCHEF.COM

MUNCH FIT

Munch Fit deliver high-quality, colourful and nutritionally balanced meals for individuals, leading gyms and businesses across London. The meals have been created using fresh seasonal ingredients, sustainable free-range produce, nutrient-rich superfoods and high-protein sources.

 MUNCHFIT.CO.UK

POTAGE

Potage delivers delicious, healthy, handmade meals that bring people together. All their food is freshly prepared by chefs each morning using the finest seasonal ingredients from local suppliers. Even their packaging has been designed with the environment in mind.

 POTAGE.CO.UK

THE PURE PACKAGE

Pure Package offers a gourmet food delivery service. They have tailored menus which cater to specific diet goals, like weight loss, detoxes and cleanses. Located right next to New Covent Garden Market, Pure Package have their pick of the best ingredients.

 PUREPACKAGE.COM

RAW FAIRIES

Raw fairies are a cleanse and raw food delivery service. Featuring only plant-based botanical goodness, they offer some seriously super cold-pressed cleanses, nut mylks and raw food.

 RAWFAIRIES.COM

RIVERFORD

Organic fruit, vegetable, meat and recipe boxes, straight from the farm to your door. With four farms across the UK, Riverford bring you quality, locally sourced ingredients.

 RIVERFORD.CO.UK

SPRING GREEN LONDON

In addition to breakfast, lunch and dinner, Spring Green offer infused botanical beauty water, a daily detox juice and a brain boosting super snack. The food is dairy-free and wheat-free and contains only natural sugars from nutrient-rich fruits.

 SPRINGGREENLONDON.COM

SPRINGBOX

A healthy and convenient meal delivery service cooked by Michelin restaurant chef, Ben Tilouche. Food to help you feel lean, fit and energetic. Dine out while you eat in, restaurant flavours using healthy ingredients.

 SPRINGBOX.ME

THE JOURNEY OF THE 'HEALTHY HIGH STREET'

BY **ALEX HEYNES,** VITAL INGREDIENT

Back in my city office job days of the mid to late 90's, I only recall the existence of just a few branded multisite lunchtime businesses. Pret and (the now defunct) Benjy's pioneered the sector in the mid 80's. EAT and Yo Sushi made an appearance in the late 90's. Whilst Pret talked about their natural food with no nasty stuff added (which of course was true), there was no operator offering and claiming to offer actively healthy food at this time.

The UK market had not yet clicked about eating healthier food like it had in Sydney for example, but the likes of Pret certainly did a bar raising job of setting new standards of food quality, store environment and service, which was welcomed by city office workers with open arms. Pret's claims of good clean food and wonderful happy staff were certainly not debatable. The founder of Pret, Julian Metcalfe, was the true pioneer of the branded lunchtime food retail sector here in London.

By the 90's, London workers could eat what they wanted to eat, be it sandwiches, prepared salads, sushi or gourmet soup, all prepared to a consistently high standard and served up by extremely well-trained and cheerful staff.

A handful of branded operators stormed the London high street without fear of competition, and soon the streets were crowded with options for Londoners looking for a quick, healthy lunch.

Even across the pond in the US, the beautifully packaged, honed and branded multisite lunchtime food operator didn't exist at the end of the last century when these new branded food outlets were in full swing in London. However, something that did exist in some of the larger US and Australian cities were independent single outlet businesses that focussed on healthy eating as their mantra. Millennial Londoners may remember Cranks. Cranks was great on paper, but it was way ahead of its time. It wasn't practical or easy enough to be mainstream, it was too expensive, and ultimately it was just a bit 'brown' and uncool. The US was full of variations of Cranks, where Americans could dodge calories and eat high fibre, high protein organic food.

Around the early 2000s, the QSR entrepreneur realised what London needed; it needed to come up with a truly healthy food offer in a unit model that rivalled Pret in execution. Take Pret's glossy store fit, witty tone of voice and staggeringly well-trained team members, but make the offer 'actively' healthy. How to do this without creating another Cranks? Make the offer accessible and familiar, avoiding the stigma of a cranky, organic only militantly healthy menu. Thanks to a sudden surge in cooking programmes and celeb chefs on TV at the start of this century, people quickly became smart to the ways of mainstream healthy eating. Today's millennials want to know the provenance of what they put in their mouths, lapping up stories of farmer Giles from a nearby village that grows the kale in their salad. The baby boomers want to know what's in the food they eat (and what's NOT in their food), and they want to know the functional health benefits of the ingredients used. As people learned more about wellness living and the effects of superfoods (such as coconut oil and chia seeds), it became clear that they were willing to pay more for better quality and genuinely healthier food.

Following the opening of Vital Ingredient in 2001, there was a massive influx of lunchtime concepts and brands that magically combined health focused food offers with brilliantly executed service. We believe leaders of the pack are itsu, LEON, Vital Ingredient, Tossed, Chop'd, POD, PURE, Wasabi and Abokado.

The tossed to order salad concept was pioneered by Vital Ingredient, and Tossed and Chop'd followed quickly behind once it was shown that Brits would indeed eat a salad for lunch most days of the week.

Alternatively, low carb Asian inspired food was an ideal healthy cuisine to base a solid business on, with slightly differing models led by health focused and high end Itsu and its mainstream counterpart, Wasabi.

Once the health food trend was established, along came POD, LEON, Coco do Mama, and PURE with different takes on fantastic healthy hot food. They based their business models off of successful fast food chains like McDonald's and Burger King, giving customers the option to eat in or take their food on foot.

With more than 50 salad concept outlets, 400 sandwich outlets who have turned their focus onto healthier options, and 150 healthy Asian inspired outlets (not to mention all the independent start-ups dotted around the city), the choice and convenience of eating healthily on the London high street has reached staggering levels.

Whilst we all have Pret to thank for setting the standard, the many branded healthy food operators are now left to fight it out on a crowded high street. The real winner in this unfolding is the customer who now has a raft of choice of very well run outlets to find their healthy fill, and that alone has to be a good thing indeed.

FARMERS' MARKETS

ALEXANDRA PALACE FARMERS' MARKET
ALEXANDRA PALACE, MUSWELL HILL, N22 7AY

OPEN

SUN.   10:00AM - 3:00PM

⊖ ALEXANDRA PALACE

BERWICK STREET MARKET
BERWICK STREET, SOHO, W1F 8RH

OPEN

MON-SAT.   8:00AM - 6:00PM
SUN.   CLOSED

⊖ OXFORD CIRCUS

BLOOMSBURY FARMERS' MARKET
TORRINGTON SQUARE, BLOOMSBURY, WC1E 7JL

OPEN

MON-FRI.   7:00AM - 6:00PM
SAT-SUN.   8:00AM - 6:00PM

⊖ RUSSELL SQUARE

BROADWAY MARKET
BROADWAY MARKET, SOUTH HACKNEY, E8 4PH

OPEN

SAT.   9:00AM - 5:00PM

⊖ LONDON FIELDS

BROCKLEY MARKET
LEWISHAM WAY, LEWISHAM, SE4 1XL

OPEN

SAT.   10:00AM - 2:00PM

⇌ ST JOHNS RAIL

CHELSEA FARMERS' MARKET
KING'S ROAD, CHELSEA, SW3 4TZ

OPEN

SAT.   10:00AM - 4:00PM

⊖ SLOANE SQUARE

ISLINGTON FARMERS' MARKET
CHAPEL MARKET, PENTON STREET, ISLINGTON, N1 9PZ

OPEN

SUN.   10:00AM - 2:00PM

⊖ ANGEL

MALTBY MARKET
41 MALTBY STREET, BERMONDSEY, SE1 3PA

OPEN

SAT.   9:00AM - 4:00PM
SUN.   11:00AM - 4:00PM

⊖ BERMONDSEY

MARYLEBONE FARMERS' MARKET
CRAMER STREET CAR PARK, MARYLEBONE, W1U 4EW

OPEN

SAT.   10:00AM - 2:00PM

⊖ BOND STREET / BAKER STREET

NOTTING HILL FARMERS' MARKET
WATERSTONE'S CAR PARK KENSINGTON PLACE, NOTTING HILL, W8 7PP

OPEN

SAT.   9:00AM - 1:00PM

⊖ NOTTING HILL GATE

PIMLICO FARMERS' MARKET
PIMLICO ROAD, BELGRAVIA, SW1W 8UT

OPEN

SAT.   9:00AM - 1:00PM

⊖ SLOANE SQUARE

PRIMROSE HILL FARMERS' MARKET
ST PAUL'S SCHOOL, ELSWORTHY ROAD, PRIMROSE HILL, NW3 3DS

OPEN

SAT.   10:00AM - 3:00PM

⊖ CHALK FARM

REAL FOOD MARKET
KING'S CROSS SQUARE, EUSTON ROAD, KING'S CROSS, N1 9AP

OPEN

WED-FRI.   12:00AM - 7:00PM

⊖ KING'S CROSS

SOUTH KENSINGTON FARMERS' MARKET
BUTE STREET, SOUTH KENSINGTON, SW7 3EX

OPEN

SAT.   9:00AM - 2:00PM

⊖ SOUTH KENSINGTON

ST KATHARINE DOCKS GOOD FOOD MARKET
ST KATHARINE DOCKS, MARBLE QUAY, E1W 1LA

OPEN

FRI.   11:00AM - 3:00PM

⊖ TOWER HILL

BOROUGH MARKET

8 SOUTHWARK STREET, SOUTHWARK, SE1 1TL

OPEN

MON-TUE.	10:00AM - 5:00PM
	(LIMITED MARKET)
WED-THU.	10:00AM - 5:00PM
FRI.	10:00AM - 6:00PM
SAT.	8:00AM - 5:00PM
SUN.	CLOSED

BOROUGHMARKET.ORG.UK

LONDON BRIDGE

Often referred to as 'London's Larder', Borough Market is well known for its fabulous food scene. An absolute must for avid gastronomes everywhere, you'll find yourself relishing in the hustle and bustle of the area. Located just south of the river, this Southwark spot dates back to the 13th Century. Nowadays, traders, tourists and locals gather here to buy and sell anything from freshly baked bread to freshly caught fish. You'll find a fantastic variety of fruit and veg sold alongside speciality meats and some indulgent sweet treats. Spoilt for choice, there is a comprehensive selection of street stalls and restaurants from which to get your fill. Wander around and take in the electric atmosphere, the smell of artisan coffee and the cheeky little tasters given out by the vendors. The Market hall looks out onto Borough High Street and resembles a greenhouse with its glassy façade. Don't miss out on the workshops, tastings and delicious looking demonstrations that are regularly held here. Borough Market is good for your wellbeing as it's wholesome, hearty and a fun day out.

FITNESS

TOP HEALTH CLUBS

BOUTIQUE FITNESS STUDIOS

INDOOR CYCLING SPECIALISTS

YOGA

PILATES

DANCE + BARRECORE

BOXING

MARTIAL ARTS

OUTDOOR SPACES

QUIRKY WORKOUTS

RUN CLUBS

ACTIVEWEAR

HIGH STREET ACTIVEWEAR

OPEN

MON-SUN.   6:30AM - 8:00PM

 CLUB.BODYISM.COM

 NOTTING HILL GATE

BODYISM

222 WESTBOURNE GROVE, NOTTING HILL, W11 2RH

Known to be a regular celebrity hotspot, Bodyism is a private members' health club in trendy Notting Hill. If it's not models and actors discreetly strolling through the door, it's high-flying businessmen and their glamorous wives. Whether they've come for one-on-one yoga, facial stretching or perhaps one of the intimate group workouts, they'll always be greeted by name on arrival. This intimacy is a breath of fresh air in the sprawling city of London, though the specially installed oxygen filters may also have something to do with it. A bespoke session with one of Bodyism's performance specialists in the functional training studio will have you squatting like an A-lister. The workouts are based on the founder James Duigan's 'Clean and Lean' method so you're likely to leave having toned muscles that previously didn't exist. For those jetsetters among us, Bodyism outposts can also be found in Capri, The Maldives and Turkey - we lycra that!

BODYWORKSWEST

11 LAMBTON PLACE, NOTTING HILL, W11 2SH

OPEN

MON-FRI. 6:15AM - 10:45PM
SAT-SUN. 8:00AM - 9:00PM

 BODYWORKSWEST.CO.UK

 NOTTING HILL GATE

This boutique members' health club is tucked discreetly into a muse just off Westbourne Grove. Established in 2008, the club offers West Londoners a chance to relax and unwind in a refreshingly calm environment. Perhaps it's the serene blue of the swimming pool, or the bespoke nature of the small group reformer Pilates classes, but BodyWorksWest draws in a glam yet understated crowd. The open plan gym has all the necessary machinery needed to get the heart rate pumped up, but it's the helpful fitness professionals that come by and offer to correct any misinformed movements that will put you in line (for the full membership). With classes that range from SUNride to aqua barre and body conditioning, the variety here will do more than keep you moving. Should you be in recovery mode from an injury, or simply a late night, BodyWorksWest also offers a key range of treatments and therapies like reflexology, physiotherapy or even cupping. But first, jacuzzi anyone?

OPEN

MON-THU.	9:00AM - 8:00PM
FRI.	9:00AM - 7:00PM
SAT.	9:00AM - 6:00PM
SUN.	9:00AM - 5:00PM

 HARBOURCLUB.COM

 IMPERIAL WHARF RAIL

THE CHELSEA HARBOUR CLUB

WATERMEADOW LANE, IMPERIAL WHARF, CHELSEA HARBOUR, SW6 2RW

Where yummy mummies reign supreme. That said, The Chelsea Harbour Club has something for everyone; whether you're looking to play a game of tennis on one of their 12 indoor tennis courts, swim in one of their 3 swimming pools or be pampered in their serene Aveda spa, it's on offer. The Chelsea Harbour Club gym is state-of-the-art. While you might struggle to keep up with their latest stair climbing machine and the super-svelte models training next to you, the extensive stretching area has private training pods that allow for a coveted escape. Even the restaurant and bar have a dedicated kids' area, decked out with a snazzy play crèche to ensure weary parents get that all important me-time. As the evening approaches, the suits stroll in and the fancy smoothies change to fruity cocktails. Treat yourself to a PT session, a relaxing steam, and get your dry cleaning done on site, surely this is what wellness is all about?

EMBODY FITNESS

1 BARTHOLOMEW LANE, THE CITY, EC2N 2AX

OPEN

MON-FRI.	6:30AM - 8:00PM
SAT.	9:00AM - 4:00PM
SUN.	CLOSED

 EMBODYFITNESS.CO.UK

 BANK

Seeking out an ultra luxury workout zone? Embody Fitness is an Olympic-standard, results driven training facility in the heart of Bank. Newly refurbished, the sleek, white space is minimal with a polished gleam of success, so nothing can distract you from your goals. Centred around a one on one personal training ethos, all packages on offer at this gym also include sports therapy and nutrition, so you can adopt an all-encompassing approach to training. You'll be assessed by a nutritionist and given a bespoke plan, and a sports therapist to identify injuries and potential problem areas, so you can work with, not against, your body. The beating heart of the venue is its personal trainers, and their undisputed credentials. The team includes former Team GB Olympians Sarah Claxton (hurdles) and Martyn Bernard (high jump), as well as 'human flag' Instagram legend, Greg Cornthwaite. It doesn't come cheap, but this fitness emporium in London's financial district is hard to beat if you're looking for expert strength and conditioning in a focused, inspirational environment. And an added bonus: all PT sessions come with a complimentary protein shake. Enjoy!

EQUINOX

5TH FLOOR, THE ROOF GARDENS, KENSINGTON HIGH STREET, KENSINGTON, W8 5SA

OPEN

MON-FRI.   6:00AM - 10:00PM

SAT-SUN.   8:00AM - 10:00PM

🌐 EQUINOX.COM

⊖ HIGH STREET KENSINGTON

Equinox is not simply a gym, it's a lifestyle. Membership to this high-end health and fitness club brings with it a whole host of alluring perks. With a class schedule to rival your Christmas wish list, Equinox offer over 120 classes per week with everything from Boxing Bootcamp, Ballet Barre Workout and Best Butt Ever, to Ab Lab, Precision Running and Tabata. The choice might feel overwhelming, but that's where the meditation sessions come in handy! Though we hasten to add, they don't do 'fads', they do what's been scientifically proven to work. In addition to their main studio, they have a boxing studio, a cycling studio, a yoga studio, a treadmill area, a spa and a room for Reformer Pilates. And we've yet to mention their state-of-the-art gym floor. It's here that you might find yourself working out next to world-class rugby players, ultra-fit financiers or the yummiest mummies around. There's an activewear shop to make sure you sweat in style, as well as a lounge area that has Wi-Fi as strong as the coffee. With a crèche for the kids, your time is your own again. Make Equinox your second home.

OPEN

MON–FRI.	6:30AM - 10:00PM
SAT.	8:00AM - 7:00PM
SUN.	9:00AM - 7:00PM

 GRACEBELGRAVIA.COM

KNIGHTSBRIDGE

GRACE BELGRAVIA

11C WEST HALKIN STREET, BELGRAVIA, SW1X 8JL

Don't just take our word for it that this women's-only spa, gym and health club really is something special in the world of wellness - look at its luxurious facilities, its restaurant and the medical clinic on-site. Co-founded by Dr Tim Evans (the Queen's doctor) and Kate Percival, health and comfort are at the core of this club. Members have the chance to discover Grace's weight optimisation programmes, juice cleanses, body bootcamps, as well as cultural evening talks and events. It's a space where women can relax and unwind, as well as network, conduct meetings and get in shape. Only on a tour around do you realise the extent of this beautiful space; its relaxed vibe, stylish charm and tasteful colour palette consistent throughout. Men are allowed to the restaurant and bar by invite-only before 9.30am and after 6.30pm. With some of the best specialists from around the world in areas like acupuncture, gynaecology, nutrition and emotional health, appointments in the clinic can also be booked by non-members - hallelujah!

GYMBOX

100 HIGH HOLBORN, HOLBORN, WC1V 6RD

OPEN

MON-FRI.   6:00AM - 11:00PM

SAT-SUN.   10:00AM - 6:00PM

 GYMBOX.COM

 HOLBORN

GYMBOX does to the gym what tinsel does to the Christmas tree; they jazz it up, give it purpose and make it easy to celebrate what most people view as mundane. Based in what used to be an underground carpark, the Holborn GYMBOX is to a serious fitness fanatic what an adventure playground is to a small child. The fact it calls itself 'the melting pot of fitness insanity' arguably says it all. The DJs spinning music from their decks, the neon glow and the dimmed down lighting sets a party tone that, in addition to the quality of equipment, the number of 'Very Personal Trainers' and the range of innovative classes, suggests a real dedication to providing a fitness experience that's anything but boring. Edgier than the boxing ring that sits in the middle of the gym floor, expect to see sweat drip from hipster beards and tattoos practically melt during the indoor cycling class, 'Tour de Holborn'. Alternatively, should you feel like reverting to your 13-year-old self at the school disco, head to the Rave class. Here you'll be given artistic licence to let those limbs loose on mini trampolines (glow sticks and wild dance moves also provided).

KX LIFE

151 DRAYCOTT AVENUE, CHELSEA, SW3 3AL

OPEN

MON-FRI.	6:30AM - 10:30PM
SAT.	8:00AM - 10:30PM
SUN.	8:00AM - 8:00PM

 KXLIFE.CO.UK

SOUTH KENSINGTON

Welcome to the world of the fast and flashy. KX Life is a private members' health and lifestyle club that combines training, nutrition and relaxation. With a premium gym, as well as a restaurant and spa, those looking for sleek and chic have come to the right place. The clientele here are likely to have just flown in from Switzerland, St. Moritz or St. Barts and whether they want the Green and Lean Juice from the KX restaurant, a one-on-one aerial yoga session, or an Oxygen Intraceutical Infusion facial in the spa, they can get it. The rich mahogany colour scheme of this club gives it a classic yet timeless feel. It's as aesthetically pleasing to the eye as the svelte bodies that saunter out of the snazzy indoor cycling studio. You can revitalize with a plunge pool, a steam room, or a sauna (perhaps all three) after one of their high-energy fitness classes. The changing rooms come with your own gown, slippers and Mani Pedi bar, but membership also comes with a premium price tag. It's indulgent and exclusive, but what better investment than one in yourself?

THE SOUTH KENSINGTON CLUB

38 - 42 HARRINGTON ROAD, KENSINGTON, SW7 3ND

OPEN

MON-FRI.   6:45AM - 12:00AM
SAT.   8:00AM - 12:00AM
SUN   11:00AM - 11:00PM

 SOUTHKENSINGTONCLUB.COM

 SOUTH KENSINGTON

Walking into the South Kensington Club, it feels a bit like you've stumbled through the wardrobe and into Narnia - another world exists behind those discreet doors on Harrington Road. What used to be Francis Bacon's house is now an extremely lush members-only "wellness and health sanctuary". Offering Turkish hammams, Russian banyas and even a saltwater watsu pool (with seawater imported from Sicily no less). This club also has a first-class gym on the top floor, hot saunas and a daily timetable

of classes ranging from Vinyasa Yoga to Booty Burn. Offering an extremely premium and exclusive experience, this club takes matters of healing, health and wellness extremely seriously.

THIRD SPACE

16 - 19 CANADA SQUARE, CANARY WHARF, E14 5ER

OPEN

MON-FRI.   5:30AM - 10:30PM
SAT.   8:00AM - 10:00PM
SUN.   10:00AM - 8:00PM

 THIRDSPACE.LONDON

 CANARY WHARF

Surrounded by gleaming, glass skyscrapers within London's ultra-modern centre of commerce, Third Space's attention-grabbing façade is a beacon of health and fitness. With three floors, 100,000 square feet of luxury training space and over 210 classes per week, you'll be spoilt for choice whatever your training style. Try classic classes like Hardcore Cycle, Boxing and Hot Pilates to get endorphins rushing, or if you're feeling more adventurous, give a signature Third Space workout a go - 'Afterburner' being a popular choice. Post-workout, there's plenty more to look forward to - unwind and rejuvenate in the luxury spa or take a dip in the 23-metre,

purified pool. Quick, healthy food is available at the Natural Fitness Food Café, or go all out with a meal and a cocktail in the grand Pearson Room.

TRANSITION ZONE

17 HEATHMAN'S ROAD, FULHAM, SW6 4TJ

OPEN
SEE WEBSITE FOR TIMETABLE

 TRANSITIONZONE.CO.UK

 PARSONS GREEN

This white, black and yellow studio looks like bootcamp. "If it doesn't challenge you...it doesn't change you," black writing scrolls across the wall. Transition Zone stays true to its name; it's all about making a positive lifestyle change. Holistic services, from classes, to massage, to nutrition make it easy. With TRX ropes dangling from a large frame, punch bags, battle ropes and power plates, the studio is fully kitted out. Classes are focused, with between four and ten slots, so the high-energy trainers can zone in on you (no slacking). TRX is ideal for those with weight bearing issues; as technical and flexible as it is power based, it's a tough full-body session, but your joints don't pay. If you're time-poor, take a 25-minute power plate class. You'll skip, squat and flick battle ropes on the vibrating plate; stimulating your muscles to contract multiple times per second, it's an ultra effective workout in half the time. HiPer Zone is a next-generation workout exclusive to Transition Zone. Choose from endurance, speed or power classes, and state-of-the-art heart rate technology will monitor your performance as you improve. The Recovery Bar offers freshly made juices, protein shakes and health shots, as well as snacks made twice weekly by a nutritionist, to help you on your way.

VIRGINACTIVE.CO.UK

BARBICAN / ST PAUL'S

THE VIRGIN ACTIVE COLLECTION

200 ALDERSGATE STREET, BARBICAN, EC1A 4HD

Step inside the quiet atrium opposite the Museum of London, descend into the spacious gym floor below, and discover an energising environment dedicated to defining and smashing your fitness goals. The gym is packed with classic and revolutionary fitness equipment designed to challenge and tone every inch of the body. Looking to develop your strengths away from the machines, or give your workout a social edge? Virgin Active Collection clubs offer a huge range of classes, from staples like Pilates and Circuit Training to the hugely popular Body Pump and Barre powered by Bootybarre. This is the perfect venue to try something a bit different too. Perhaps you're an accomplished yogi looking to strengthen your asanas? Find your Zen while swaying a few feet from the floor with Anti-Gravity Yoga - sure to work your core like never before. Light refreshments and complimentary tea and coffee are available in the Members Lounge for a quick post-workout refuel, and round off your visit with a trip to the club's tranquil pool or luxury spa.

109

GOAL SETTING

BY **WILL DANIELS, TIER X COACH,** EQUINOX KENSINGTON

Goal setting is important because goals create new habits that can have a positive long-term impact on your state of wellness.

KNOW YOURSELF, WHAT MOTIVATES YOU

Goal setting can be daunting - you may be unsure how to approach the process, thinking that you have never set a goal before, or you may doubt your ability to achieve your goal. It's important to recognize that you are in fact capable! Look at previous successes in your life that are not wellness related, like a promotion, a pay rise, learning a new skill, deciding to move house or a new job. What did you do to achieve success? You might be surprised to find that you've already gone through the process of goal setting in the past, even if you didn't sit down and formally work it out.

HOW TO SET GOALS

Before setting a goal, you should embark on a period of self-reflection. Now is the time to pause and ask yourself these questions: what do I want to do? What actionable steps can I take? And, what is currently getting in my way of achieving this? This is a chance to look for areas of opportunity within your lifestyle, considering your own level of readiness, willing and ability, to set your goals and commit to them.

Once you've looked at the changes you want to make, it's time to set your goal. No goal is more important than another - it could be as ambitious as running a marathon or as simple as getting more sleep.

LET'S GET PERSONAL

You now have to ask yourself a big deep and meaningful, "WHY?" When you answer one question, ask yourself why again, think of it as peeling back the layers of an onion. This is likely to create a lightbulb moment, and it may surprise you as asking yourself "why", is the most important way for you to connect yourself with the goal you will ultimately set.

Whatever your goal, the important motivation behind it will be answered with your period of deep reflection. Personal goal setting plays to the concept that if you have the idea, the goal, you're more likely to implement it. Don't set a goal that you have read in a magazine - try to make it more personal.

HAVING A VISION

When you have done your searching and are confident in your why, it's time to commit to your goal. If it's "I want to feel fitter and have more energy," write this down and write down why. Think how you will feel when you achieve this goal and write that down too.

Use this piece of paper to go to when you hit a bump in the road, lose motivation or feel like you could give up. This is a very powerful technique as it turns your goal into something physical and tangible - you really have to think about the words you are writing. Think of it as signing a contract, as if you would a new job or for a house lease, but this is for your health.

HOW TO MOTIVATE

Goal setting is not about giving yourself impossible tasks, it's actually about setting yourself up to be successful. If you are not quietly confident that you can set out to achieve it, it's probably too big. So this is the time to take it back a step, to shrink your goals - this does not diminish their importance, it makes them achievable.

For example, you might want to go to the gym everyday but your long work hours don't realistically allow for that. Instead, commit to three times a week and see

the other occasions where you manage some physical activity as bonuses. Then you will feel successful in what you have set out to commit to.

Another important element of goal setting is creating an accountability system of sorts. If you are not working with a personal trainer or a coach whose job is to keep you on track, you need accountability. It could be that you share your goals with a friendship group, family or partner and check in with them as you progress. Some people find it helpful to track their goals and successes through social media. A little support goes a long way when you are striving to reach your goals.

MEASURE YOUR GOALS/SUCCESS

To keep track of your successes and progress, set weekly goals. I find attributing a number to the goal ensures that it's quantifiable. An example of this would be, "I will go to bed three nights a week before midnight."

Setting a number lets you know if you are being successful or not in black and white fashion. Have I reduced my coffee intake from three a day to one a day? Can I say by the end of the week how many coffees I've had each day? If you can't, you're not assessing - you're guessing. It's vital that you check in with yourself to measure your progress.

Reaching a goal, be it running 5k, reducing your caffeine intake, or increasing your flexibility, is a great time to set another goal. Feed off that success and continue your journey to a state of better wellness!

IN CONCLUSION

Goal setting is a deeply personal process. The point of a goal is to empower and uplift. You should feel upbeat and positive about achieving something for yourself.

Tier X is a High Performance Lifestyle Management Program, available at Equinox Kensington.

equinox.com

1REBEL

63 ST MARY AXE, LIVERPOOL STREET, EC3A 8LE

OPEN

MON-SUN.   5:30AM - 9:30PM

 1REBEL.CO.UK

 LIVERPOOL STREET

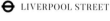

The fitness fanatics at 1Rebel call themselves 'the Rebel army', so what is it that makes them a force to be reckoned with on London's evolving fitness scene? Their St Mary Axe studio, located over two floors in the city of London, caters for the RIDE class as well as their signature RESHAPE. The RIDE is a high-energy 30 or 45 minute cycle session - a full-body workout that's often themed to give it a funky twist. Occasionally you'll be accompanied by a DJ on the decks to blast you through the burn. The RESHAPE class combines treadmill and floor work, designed to be a physically and mentally strenuous group exercise experience; walking up stairs the next day will be just as challenging! With a cold-pressed juice bar on site, as well as a blow-dry and braid bar, this is the gift that just keeps giving. The changing rooms deserve a 5* rating with their chilled towels for after class and their premium range of products. The Broadgate location plays host to their awesome RUMBLE class. Using speed, strength and footwork to beat up the hanging bags, this cardio boxing will leave you feeling like a kickass legend.

THE ALTITUDE CENTRE

6 TRUMP STREET, THE CITY, EC2V 8AF

OPEN

MON-FRI.   7:00AM - 9:00PM

SAT-SUN.   CLOSED

 ALTITUDECENTRE.COM

 BANK

One for tech lovers, the Altitude Centre is a high spec training facility close to Bank. Here, it's all about 'the chamber', a workout space with reduced oxygen levels, simulating 2,700m above sea level. Whilst the amount of air in the chamber is relative to sea level, a molecular sieve filters the oxygen levels down to around 15%, so you train as fast as at sea level, but it is harder and more beneficial. Regular exposure to high altitude dramatically brings down your recovery time. The Altitude Centre run six high intensity classes per day, where you can run, cycle or row. We

recommend trying the IHE Pod (Intense Hypoxia Exposure) - its mask simulates 6000m above sea level; by way of passive acclimatisation, there are massive overall fitness benefits, and all you're doing is sitting in a chair. High fives all round.

ANOTHER_SPACE

4 - 10 TOWER STREET, SEVEN DIALS, WC2H 9NP

OPEN

MON-FRI.   6:30AM - 9:00PM

SAT-SUN.   8:00AM - 5:00PM

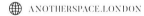 ANOTHERSPACE.LONDON

 COVENT GARDEN

As the trend for membership-free boutique fitness studios takes hold, Another_Space is one to keep an eye on. The white colour scheme has the desired effect of creating a clean and calming space. The idea behind this minimalist design is to offer "everything you need and nothing you don't" (it must be said that the changing rooms here are sublime and perfectly kitted out). In keeping with the uncluttered vibe, there is a choice of three classes; HIIT, Yoga and Cycle, making it easy to mix and match your weekly exercise regime. Unsurprisingly, (given its location in the West

End) many of the instructors have a background training in dance and musical theatre. You can't help but love the pinch of sass that inspires the classes and their accompanying soundtracks. You go gurl!

BARRY'S BOOTCAMP

163 EUSTON ROAD, EUSTON, NW1 2BH

OPEN

MON-THU.	5:45AM - 10:30PM
FRI.	5:45AM - 9:30PM
SAT.	7:00AM - 8:30PM
SUN.	7:00AM - 7:00PM

 BARRYSBOOTCAMP.COM

EUSTON

There are no excuses at Barry's Bootcamp. You turn up to turn it up and push yourself harder than you ever have before. Founded in 1998, Barry's Bootcamp has come over from LA to London and firmly established itself as a trendsetter in the burgeoning boutique fitness sphere. The classes are military style group workouts that combine equal length intervals of cardio and floor work. Over the period of an hour you will move from treadmill sprints to weight training and resistance exercises. The lights are turned down low and a hazy red glow fills the room - crop tops and six packs seem to be the general dresscode. Given the thumping music, you'd be forgiven for thinking you'd just walked in to the Oscar's afterparty. Celebrity endorsed and well known for their cult-like following, Barry's instructors live, eat and breathe the brand with their charismatic encouragement and motivational mantras. While exhaustion may creep in, your enthusiasm is not allowed to go below 100%. Can we get a high five and a 'HELL YEAH'?

BEST'S BOOTCAMP

CONCOURSE LEVEL 1, EMBANKMENT PLACE, EMBANKMENT, WC2N 6NN

OPEN

MON-FRI.	6:30AM - 8:30PM
SAT.	8:00AM - 11:00PM
SUN.	9:00AM - 12:00PM

 BESTSBOOTCAMP.COM

 EMBANKMENT

If you're looking for your abs, you're most likely to find them at Best's Bootcamp. The intensive sessions last for 50 minutes and include switching between climbs and sprints on the FreeMotion treadmill and strength training on the Best's box. Depending on the day of the week, the class will focus on lower body, upper body or full body workouts. The Trainer Cam is a particularly popular feature here, as it projects the instructor's demonstrations onto a large screen - keeping their

well-sculpted physique in full view. If Bootcamp classes aren't your thing, their BEST Cycle studio can be found downstairs (cleats provided). With hill climbs and interval sprints, these sessions are no less challenging. Strive to be the best of the Best!

CENTRIC:3TRIBES

EXCHANGE HOUSE, 71 CROUCH END HILL, CROUCH END, N8 8DF

OPEN

SEE WEBSITE FOR TIMETABLE

 3TRIBES.CO.UK

 CROUCH HILL

Don't judge a book by its cover and the same rings true for Centric3Tribes. Located just behind M&S on Crouch End Hill, the reception area is deceptively small, because downstairs the space transforms with a trendy bunker vibe. Past the juice and smoothie bar you'll find the Ride room with 30 bikes for indoor cycling (cleats provided), the Warrior room with treadmills, TRX, weights and step stations, and the Zen room for yoga and barre. Centric3Tribes mix things up with their 'Mixed Tribe Mash-Up' classes that offer 30 mins of Rider followed by 30 mins of Zen or half Warrior half Rider. Challenge accepted.

115

CORE-COLLECTIVE.CO.UK

HIGH STREET KENSINGTON

CORE COLLECTIVE

45 PHILLIMORE WALK, KENSINGTON, W8 7RZ

Tucked away on a seemingly residential road just off High Street Kensington, this hidden jewel is no secret to London's mega-fit elite. With pay-as-you-go workouts, the 4 main classes; Velocity, Resistance, Sculpt and Accelerate, vary from athletic interval training, to TRX, flexibility and straight up indoor cycling. It must be said that the indoor cycling studio is particularly chic, featuring a funky light arrangement that feels as though you've entered a life size light-up boom box. This class includes a series of performance climbs and sprints - nothing like a hard hill to get the day going. To get you back looking your best, the changing rooms come delightfully well-equipped with spacious showers, large fluffy towels, hair dryers, straighteners and well-positioned mirrors (for the perfect post-sweat selfie). Prepare to work extra hard for the dizzying array of astonishingly attractive trainers... If you can, stay cool, calm and core collective.

CROSSFIT CENTRAL LONDON

ARCH 56, 57 EWER STREET, SOUTHWARK, SE1 0NR

MON-THU.　　6:00AM - 9:00PM
FRI.　　　　 6:00AM - 8:00PM
SAT.　　　　 9:30AM - 5:00PM
SUN.　　　　 10:00AM - 3:00PM

 CROSSFITCENTRALLONDON.
CO.UK

 SOUTHWARK

CrossFit Central London is not for the faint-hearted. Combining cardio, gymnastics and weightlifting, this form of training has recently been adopted by the US Navy SEALS, the Canadian Army, Police and Special Forces worldwide - so it's bound to get you feeling ship shape, sweaty and supremely sculpted. But you don't just come here to build muscle, you come here to build friendships, community spirit and self-confidence. Put through your paces from the word go, the workouts are scalable depending on your ability, so whether you're 18 or 80, it's all doable. Fully equipped with the CrossFit gear and bespoke rigs, they offer foundation training, beginners classes, Olympic weightlifting, yoga, kettlebell classes and 'Workout of the Day' classes; no one session is designed to be the same. The peak hours are in the morning and the evening, and you are encouraged to train at least 3 times per week in order to get the most from your membership. CrossFit will show you the endorphins in endurance, and to prove it - your first taster session is free.

DIGME FITNESS

SPENCER HOUSE, 23 SHEEN ROAD, RICHMOND, TW9 1BN

'Digme' could conceivably mean a host of things, but when you learn that the name of this state-of-the-art cycle studio is taken from the name of the Kona beach, which serves as the starting line for the World Ironman Championships, you'll understand that classes here are tough. Super friendly instructors lead you through each session by microphone, and two large screens at the front simulate your ride. To help you push through, the sleek studio is pitch black with disco lights and glow in the dark bike monitors noting all of your stats. Each instructor makes their own playlists at least once a week, so the music is guaranteed to be fresh and fun. Don't miss 'Beats 'n Cleats', a themed Friday bimonthly ride, which comes complete with UV paint and a kick-ass playlist. Get ready to tackle hill climbs, time trials and group challenges, but once you've seen the sessions through, a treat awaits in the form of luxurious showers, Cowshed products and Dyson hairdryers. Grab a protein shake to go; Kona Crunch is Digme's signature.

DUO CHELSEA

2 GUNTER GROVE, CHELSEA, SW10 0UJ

OPEN

MON-FRI.   6:00AM - 9:00PM
SAT.   7:00AM - 5:00PM
SUN.   BY APPOINTMENT

🌐 DUOCHELSEA.COM

☉ FULHAM BROADWAY

Small and compact, DUO Chelsea do well to fit so many pieces of equipment into this personal training studio just off the Fulham road. Suitable for anyone looking to up their game when it comes to weights, squats, side-jumps or kettlebell swings, this studio is designed for personal trainers to work with clients both one-on-one and in semi-PTs. The semi-PT sessions: Strong & Lean, Defcon 5-1, Primal Power and Strong Women, are kept small. 'Strong and Lean' focuses on strength training and functional movements. 'Defcon 5-1' is a 45-minute progressive HIIT class using plyometrics, indoor cycling and rowing (anything to keep you moving). 'Primal Power' is a hybrid of the former two, and 'Strong Women' centres on sculpting the physique with push, pull and lift exercises. The variety of trainers means that each class varies in style and the equipment choice changes. Though public memberships are not offered and personal training sessions are by appointment only, this is a great little find for anyone looking for a highly-personalized workout routine.

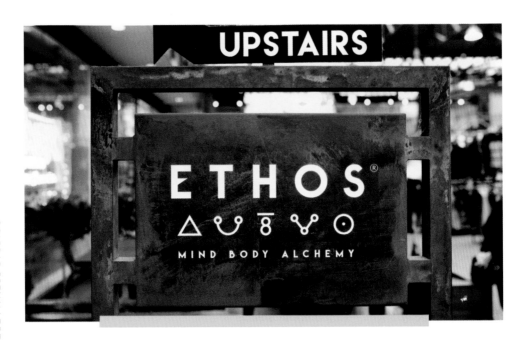

ETHOS

8 HORNER SQUARE, OLD SPITALFIELDS MARKET, SPITALFIELDS, E1 6EW

OPEN
SEE WEBSITE FOR TIMETABLE

 ETHOS.CO

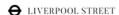 LIVERPOOL STREET

A trendy urban hybrid of yoga and fitness, ETHOS has three main studios and offers classes in tabata, TRX, yoga, indoor cycling, and barre. Located on the upper deck of Spitalfields market, ETHOS is a blessing to East London's hipsters and city workers alike, shaking up their standard gym routine. The signature 'TRX Annihilator' class is designed to have you in pieces by the end. Whatever your level or ability, this puts those monotonous 20 minutes on the cross-trainer to shame. The husband-wife duo that own ETHOS are both Cambridge graduates and have based the concept on the idea that a sacred space is needed for people to explore their own authenticity through movement. The hot yoga studio has water features around the edge and can fit up to 70 people in a class. In line with the hybrid style of the studio, the signature 'Hot Soul Flow' class fuses yoga, Pilates and dance movements in a sequence set to music. It's the variety of style in each class that will keep you coming back; it's the 'Mind, Body, Alchemy' magic.

EVOLVE 353

353 NEW KING'S ROAD, FULHAM, SW6 4RJ

OPEN

MON-FRI.	6:45AM - 8:00PM
SAT.	9:00AM - 11:00AM
SUN.	CLOSED

🌐 EVOLVE353.COM

⊖ PUTNEY BRIDGE

Evolve 353 is still a comparatively new kid on the New Kings Road. Set up by experienced trainers Ashton Turner and David Arnot as a joint venture, this dual-floor studio strips back any unnecessary frills and offers a refreshingly gimmick-free fitness experience. The walls are left bare besides the odd motivational quote like "no pain, no champagne" and #evolvetogether to remind the class why they've hauled themselves out of bed and onto machines like the Nordic ski trainer at some crazy hour in the morning. While the 'Sculpt' class focusses on resistance exercises, the 'Ignite' session works on cardio vascular conditioning; both use high intensity interval training to get the body burning fat in a fast and efficient manner. The option of private and semi-private classes are available for anyone looking to ramp up their workout routine, but get ready to squat, drop and flex to compete with Evolve's devilishly high standards.

EXERCEO TRAINING

18 ALIE STREET, WHITECHAPEL, E1 8DE

OPEN

SEE WEBSITE FOR TIMETABLE

 EXERCEOTRAINING.CO.UK

 PARSONS GREEN

This style of training is fast, efficient and well worth the short amount of time you need to spend there. They say you'll achieve the same results in 25 minutes, as 90 minutes of conventional training. The Exerceo sessions work wonders for the time-starved Londoners of today. You don't even need to remember to pack your gym gear as leggings and a top are provided! During the session, a futuristic-looking body suit is worn and this enables the electrical impulses to spread to certain parts of the body, honing in on your muscle groups to make them work harder while you repeat a range of function movements like squats, side-jumps and sit-ups. The strange sensation of the electrical impulses does take a moment to get used to, but there's no doubt it does the job. Said to burn 500 calories per session and up to 3000 over a 48 hour period, it's no surprise that Exerceo Training see themselves as the future of fitness.

F45 TRAINING TOTTENHAM COURT ROAD

114 - 115 TOTTENHAM COURT ROAD, BLOOMSBURY, W1T 5AH

OPEN

SEE WEBSITE FOR TIMETABLE

 F45TRAINING.CO.UK

 WARREN STREET

F45 is one of the world's fastest-growing workout franchises, but clearly Londoners are only just catching on to this Aussie-inspired, team-orientated training concept. There are times for small group exercise but this is not one of them. It's all about the amount you put in being equal to the amount you get out - so a full class helps to get the momentum in full swing, and swing you will when it comes to the jack hammer. These 45-minute sessions are based around exercises done in sets of short timed intervals. The room is set up to accommodate easy movement between the different pieces of equipment - ropes, kettlebells, rowing machines, sleds, swiss balls - you name it, they've got it. In case you forget what you're meant to be doing next, each station is demonstrated on the television screen clearly in view. The trainer paces round to remind you, that if you're not struggling, you're not challenging yourself. This circuits-based system gets you moving in every which way and to keep you stimulated, it's different every day.

THE FOUNDRY

BLACK PRINCE COMMUNITY HUB, 5 BEAUFOY WALK, LAMBETH, SE11 6HU

OPEN

SEE WEBSITE FOR TIMETABLE

 FOUNDRYFIT.CO.UK

 KENNINGTON

Navigating through the rather ominous looking council estate to get to the Black Prince Community Hub is at first a little daunting, but on arrival it's clear that The Foundry is the real deal - a ruby in the rubble. What used to be a gym hall has been cleverly converted into a space to build body strength. The amount of muscle building equipment around the periphery of the hall may well have trained the Spartan army. One of the founders, Ben

Gotting told us The Foundry was set up "to empower both men and women to feel strong and confident in themselves". This gym is by no means glamorous, but the no-nonsense approach to training has a refreshing air of authenticity. Real people getting real results. Try the City Strongman class to put your triceps to the test.

FRAME

4 BRIDGE PLACE, VICTORIA, SW1V 1JZ

OPEN

MON-FRI.   6:45AM - 8:30PM

SAT-SUN.   9:00AM - 5:00PM

 MOVEYOURFRAME.COM

 VICTORIA

In recent years, Victoria has undergone a rapid transformation, and with it comes one of the latest and greatest of London's boutique fitness studios, FRAME. Only a 20 second walk away from Victoria station, it's perfectly located for commuters and locals alike. This boutique fitness gym seems to have locations popping up all over London and offers high-quality classes in dance, barre, Pilates, fitness, meditation, mumhood pre and post-natal, and yoga. The range and diversity of the schedule is part of the fun, as is the multi-coloured colour scheme that simply exudes an upbeat aura. The Victoria location has 3 studios including reformer Pilates, yoga/Barre and a soundproof

fitness studio, so there's always a class on the go. With names like: Music Video, FRAME Rave, Cardio Circuits, FRAME Barre and FRAME Lift, every class has its own unique twist. Fuel at FRAME serves protein bowls, protein pancakes and super shakes, an easy spot to catch up with fellow FRAMErs after class. And if you ever forget your gear, they've got a 'forgot your kit' kit for hire - Hallelujah!

GOOD VIBES STUDIOS

14 - 16 BETTERTON STREET, COVENT GARDEN, WC2H 9BU

OPEN

MON-WED.	7:30AM - 8:30PM
THU.	7:30AM - 8:00PM
FRI.	7:30AM - 7:00PM
SAT.	10:00AM - 5:15PM
SUN.	11:00AM - 5:30PM

🌐 GOODVIBESFITNESS.CO.UK

🚇 COVENT GARDEN

Good Vibes have two central London locations, one in Fitzrovia and the other in Covent Garden. The Covent Garden studio can be found on Betterton Street and offers a combination of classes that range from Power Plates: HIIT to Glow Pilates. The Glow Cycle classes involve a high-intensity, low-impact workout for 35 minutes to an hour and their lunchtime sessions provide the perfect opportunity to swap computers for cardio and jump aboard a bike. But if that's not your training of choice, the yoga

studio is bright and welcoming and instructors practise a variety of styles that can leave you feeling anywhere from strong and sweaty to rejuvenated and restored, a good chance to balance out your yang with some yin.

GYMCLASS

168 HOLLAND PARK AVENUE, HOLLAND PARK, W11 4UH

OPEN

MON-SUN.	6:00AM - 9:30PM

🌐 GYM-CLASS.CO.UK

🚇 SHEPHERD'S BUSH

This Holland Park fitness haven looks every bit a glamorous version of military bootcamp. The studio is fitted with orange monkey bar frames, and lined with kettlebells and dumbbells, ready for action. GymClass is the concept of fitness expert, Helle Hammonds and it lives up to its claim as a world leader in group fitness. Choose your class based on the body part you want to sculpt, Ass + Abs to Full Body and everything in-between. Before you know it, you'll be squatting, ducking into burpees, and sweat will pour. The trainers won't give you time to stop and think - no breaks - you'll just

be working out like your life depends on it. At GymClass, hardcore is fun and fun is hardcore.

126

KOBOX

122 KING'S ROAD, CHELSEA, SW3 4TR

OPEN

MON-FRI.   6:15AM - 8:30PM
SAT-SUN.   8:00AM - 6:00PM

 KOBOXLONDON.COM

 SLOANE SQUARE

We came, we saw, we KOBOXed. This boutique boxing studio just off the King's Road is where "FIGHTCLUB meets NIGHTCLUB"- imagine Mohammed Ali in Ibiza and you might get more of an idea. Based on a mixture of heavy bag boxing and functional strength training, the instructor will take you from upper cuts to burpees and back again in no time at all. Using short, sharp intervals, the hanging bag punch sequence is signalled by numbers projected onto the wall. This, along with the rollicking beats, make it hard to lose your groove. The room is dimly lit with UV lights so if you're bold and feeling feisty, make sure to wear some neon gear to strut your stuff. For first timers, arrive early to get your bearings and your KOBOX customised wraps! Be ready to throw medicine balls, box jump, pull and push resistance bands and lift free weights. KOBOX is the perfect place for anyone looking to relieve tension, challenge the mind, sculpt the body and boost self-defence. KOBOX also have a studio in The City... Ding! Ding! Ding!

LOMAX

293 FULHAM ROAD, CHELSEA, SW10 9PZ

OPEN

MON-FRI.   6:00AM - 9:00PM

SAT-SUN.   9:00AM - 5:00PM

 LOMAXPT.COM

 GLOUCESTER ROAD

You'll certainly be put through your paces at LOMAX Chelsea. With 12 fitness pods, a reformer Pilates studio and an indoor cycling studio, this place prides itself on offering fitness 'The Lomax Way'. Combine the pay-as-you-go exercise, nutrition plans and wellbeing therapies to get you in sizzling shape. The Blast Class is their signature, using a mixture of high-intensity activity with compound weightlifting and full bodyweight exercises - expect short bursts of press ups, burpees, squats, deadlifts and lunges. The founder and CEO,

Jonathan Lomax, is himself a sought after personal trainer at the gym. Refusing to let people get complacent with boring gym machines, he is particularly renowned for his brilliant variety of full body workout sessions. Ladies, form an orderly queue.

METHOD

249 OLD BROMPTON ROAD, CHELSEA, SW5 9HP

OPEN

MON-FRI.   6:00AM - 9:00PM

SAT.   8:00AM - 6:00PM

SUN.   8:30AM - 6:00PM

 METHODMOVEMENT.CO.UK

 EARL'S COURT

METHOD focusses on getting tangible results. Founder and head trainer Joshua Clark puts progression and community at the heart of each class, as well as each personalised transformation programme. This basement studio, super close to Earl's court station, is beautifully designed and offers Yoga, Barre and HIIT. With its natural sunlight and signature METHOD illustrations intricately drawn on the walls, you've likely seen this spot on Instagram. Using fitness tools to tell a story, each kettlebell has a different Maori tribal symbol on, so you're made to lift 'courage', 'protection' or

'strength', not just heavy metal. Their outdoor yoga studio is referred to as 'the mindful garden', with a retractable roof for summer as well as infrared heaters on colder days - the term 'sanctuary' springs to mind. We'll see you there for the Bondi Method class!

MINISTRY DOES FITNESS

ARCHES 80 - 81, NEWINGTON COURT, ELEPHANT AND CASTLE, SE1 6DD

OPEN

MON-WED.	6.00AM - 10:00AM | 5:00PM - 9.00PM
THU-FRI.	6.00AM - 10:00AM | 5:00PM - 11.00PM
SAT.	9:00AM - 1:00PM
SUN.	CLOSED

MINISTRYDOESFITNESS.COM

ELEPHANT AND CASTLE

When an institution of British club culture turns its head to fitness, you know it won't be conventional. Enter Ministry of Fitness - tucked inside The Arches behind Ministry of Sound, this boisterous venue is bringing a new social fitness movement to the city. The lobby doubles up as a trendy bar (think exposed brickwork, rustic wood and chalkboards), and is decked out in true Ministry style with a DJ set and drinks menu - choose your post-workout shake or mocktail (with names like 'Bitch Don't Kale My Vibe', how can you say no?). Each day has a different workout theme: Monday is Cardio, Tuesday is Strength etc. and there are two instructors present per class. Sessions are an addictive mix of high-intensity interval training and adrenaline-pumping nightclub funk, complete with London's 'freshest beats'. It's not as daunting as it sounds - Ministry of Fitness is popular with fitness novices and addicts alike. Hurry up and get involved.

OPEN

MON-FRI.	6:00AM - 10.30PM
SAT-SUN.	7:00AM - 9:00PM

 ONELDN.COM

 IMPERIAL WHARF RAIL

ONE LDN

IMPERIAL WHARF, THE BOULEVARD, CHELSEA HARBOUR, SW6 2UB

What are you looking for? Muay-Thai? Boxing? HIIT? Cycle? A seriously snazzy fighting cage? Well, One LDN has specialist classes and facilities to suit. This impressive Imperial Wharf gym has five studios: one for Cycle, one for Flex and Core, one for Strength and Conditioning, one for Muay Thai and Boxing, the other for HIIT. They also have a gym floor with a large free weights area and a multitude of hi-tech machines to choose from. Tech geeks will love how their equipment is linked to the latest cloud technology, allowing users to sync and track their workout in the fitness app of their choice. Not only do members reap the benefits of cross-training in so many different activities, they can also monitor their body composition, measurements and nutrition to enhance performance levels and potentially weight loss. The pay-as-you-go classes get cheaper the more you attend, but there is also the option of an 'All you can eat classes and gym' membership. Who else is hungry for HIIT?

PERPETUA FITNESS

74 QUEEN'S CIRCUS, 326 - 342 QUEENSTOWN ROAD, BATTERSEA, SW8 4NE

OPEN

MON-FRI.   6:00AM - 8:30PM
SAT.   8:00AM - 12:30PM
SUN.   11:00AM - 12:30PM

 CROSSFITPERPETUA.COM

 BATTERSEA PARK RAIL

People don't simply dabble in CrossFit, they commit. It's not just about training, it's about mental strength, agility and hard work. But this hard work gets results, especially if you've signed up to CrossFit Perpetua and you're looking to partake in what's often referred to as 'the sport of fitness'. Found in two renovated railway arches right beside Battersea park, Perpetua Fitness has high ceilings, natural light and all the gear to get you sweaty in seconds. Doing more work in less time, the focus here is on functional movements that come naturally. Working on your core control, here you'll never see isolated movements because it's about building up your body as a whole. To get started, their fundamentals program is compulsory and teaches you 35 to 40 key movements. It is in these starter sessions that your allocated coach works with you to determine your individual needs and goals, whilst simultaneously preparing you for the group classes. Their slogan reads 'Home of the Unbroken', a reference to the community ethos within this fitness hub.

PROJECT FIT

36 - 38 CORNHILL, THE CITY, EC3V 3NG

OPEN

MON-FRI.   6:00AM - 9:00PM
SAT.   9:00AM - 3:00PM
SUN.   CLOSED

 PROJECT-FIT.CO.UK

 BANK

This calorie-crunching urban fitness Mecca has one simple motto: "You vs your body." Project Fit's innovative interval training workouts are designed to shock the body. The gym specialises in 45-minute workouts run by one of six trainers; half of each session is spent running and half doing floor work. Claiming to burn up to 750 calories in 45 minutes, this is one serious body transformation gym. Built to be an inclusive, non-judgemental space, their 'walker - jogger - runner' system, ensures all abilities can join classes, tailoring

the experience to each gym-goer. State-of-the art lighting, an urban warehouse feel, and a live DJ for special events mean you'll be at one with the hype, but we won't pretend that getting back up the stairs post-session is easy.

THE REFINERY

14 COLLENT STREET, HACKNEY, E9 6SG

OPEN

MON-FRI.   7:00AM - 9:00PM
SAT.   9:00AM - 5:00PM
SUN.   10:00AM - 6:00PM

 THEREFINERYE9.COM

HOMERTON /
HACKNEY CENTRAL

Helmed by effervescent Zoe Bertali, The Refinery E9 is a wonderland for wellbeing. In a lantern-lit, cavern-like tunnelled out basement are the main three studios, reception, retail area and therapy rooms; one floor up is a fourth studio. Varieties of yoga, Pilates, barre and fitness classes are on offer, as well as nutritional therapy, massage and more. Studios are kept small to ensure that each class-goer gets specific attention from their teacher. From Sophie and her Disco Barre class, to Restorative Forest yoga with Ellie, and AAA: Ass-Arms-Abs with 'push mind over body' Marlon, The Refinery

has a highly inclusive approach, designed to make everyone feel welcome. For a weird-but-wonderful experience, try Gong Bath, a deep relaxation and sound healing class. Change your routine to change your perception.

SLICE URBAN FITNESS

11 HEATHMAN'S ROAD, FULHAM, SW6 4TJ

OPEN

MON–FRI.   6:45AM – 9:30PM

SAT.   6:45AM – 3:00PM

SUN.   6:45AM – 1:30PM

 SLICESTUDIOS.CO.UK

 PARSONS GREEN

Just a few minutes' walk from Parsons Green station, Slice Urban Fitness is constantly abuzz with lycra-clad class-goers flowing into and out of the door. With around 120 classes per week, each in one of four studios, they offer a huge variety of activities in a social setting - from basic Pilates, to trampoline rebounding and box fit. Barre Conditioning is a Slice specialty that works to develop lean muscles by using high repetition and full-range movements, with focus on posture, core, flexibility and balance. An obvious hit in the run up to summer is Bikini

Body Workout, a hardcore, results-based body buster that incorporates an immense 90 minutes of high-energy fat-melting cardio with body strength. This is a functional yet chic studio, ideal for busy Londoners looking to stay fit in a fun environment.

STUDIO LAGREE

35 - 37 CHISWELL STREET, BARBICAN, EC1Y 4SE

OPEN

MON–FRI.   6:00AM – 10:00PM

SAT–SUN.   9:00AM – 2:00PM

 STUDIOLAGREEUK.COM

 MOORGATE / BARBICAN

One for hard core gym-lovers, this studio claims to offer the hottest workout from Hollywood. Studio Lagree offers London a high octane, bootcamp-style workout. Located in a basement, the studio is equipped with the M3 Megaformer™, Lagree's patented machine and the centre of action for the signature M3 Fusion Class. The 50-minute workout is uniquely designed to test every ounce of your core, endurance, cardio, balance, strength and flexibility. Despite its body busting credentials, M3 Fusion is a no-impact program, making it ideal for those with weight-bearing issues or injuries

who still want to participate in exciting classes. A little hype goes a long way, and blazing disco strobes, vibrating bass and the microphone-amplified motivational instruction of the trainer will have you pulling on the handles and straps with all your might. Good luck.

THE TRAIN STATION GYM

20 - 22 JAGGARD WAY, WANDSWORTH COMMON, SW12 8SG

OPEN

MON-FRI.	6:00AM - 9:00PM
SAT.	8:00AM - 12:00PM
SUN	8:45AM - 11:00AM

🌐 THETRAINSTATIONGYM.CO.UK

⇌ WANDSWORTH COMMON RAIL

If you're looking to ramp up your workout routine, attending a class at The Train Station will certainly put you on the right track. Located in a large warehouse-style space right next to Wandsworth Common train station, this trainer-led facility offers a variety of group fitness, indoor cycling, yoga, performance preparation and one-on-one training options. Its position next to the park, as well as the huge doors that open out to let in the sun, make it an especially popular choice for those that live locally and can jog home across the common. Though the proximity to the station makes it an equally easy option for commuters to do an early morning session and then dash to work. Fittingly, the signature class is called 'The Junction'- a hybrid session designed to work on functional movement, strength, conditioning and cardiovascular. But if you're not up for that, the 'Yummy Mummies' class takes life a little easier - babies and dogs amusingly watch on as the sit-ups and side-planks take place.

UN1T

132 WANDSWORTH BRIDGE ROAD, FULHAM, SW6 2UL

There is no 'I' in team, nor is there an 'I' in UN1T. This Fulham gym is based around the mantra 'we train as one' which means that the exercises are carried out in pairs and the workouts are not only about pushing yourself, but also your partner. The studio itself is a sleek monochrome and kitted out with a variety of functional fitness equipment. The classes are circuits-based and specially designed to develop your strength, mobility and cardio. Varying from 45 minutes to an hour long, the sessions are structured around timed intervals at each station. Prepare to move from kettlebells to resistance bands, on to isokinetic air bikes and squat jumps on repeat. The classes will vary in their focus depending on whether you choose: Entity, Legion, Trooper, Force, Regiment or Grind, but while the equipment might change, the emphasis on team mentality doesn't. There is also a studio for Dynamic Yoga which lets you stretch out those hard-worked muscles. Train the body, train the mind. Go team, go!

SMASH HIT

BY **CLAIRE FINLAY,** TRANSITION ZONE

WHAT IS HIT?

If you've only got half an hour to exercise, you want to make damn sure you're getting the most out of every minute. How? With high intensity training. HIT is the last word in results-driven fitness and one of the most effective ways to burn fat. Loved by athletes and lauded by celebrities, it involves short bursts of intense exercise with brief periods of either active recovery or complete rest in between.

HIT can be applied to pretty much any discipline, from cardio to conditioning, boxing to burpees. The beauty is anything goes, but to make it effective you need to make absolutely sure you're working to full capacity. As long as you get your heart pumping, HIT provides an exceptional workout in a very short space of time.

Increasingly busy lives mean most people are time-pressed, which is why HIT workouts are garnering such popularity. Less time exercising doesn't mean you won't see dramatic results - far from it. In the right hands HIT delivers a no-holds-barred workout that burns calories, torches fat, tones muscle and leaves you feeling undeniably pumped. At Transition Zone we like to go one step further by integrating suspension straps, fitness balls, kettle bells and hand weights into our HIT sessions to make sure clients work at peak performance.

In a world where we're time-poor and looking for the most effective workout possible in the shortest time, HIT has many of the answers. You can get a full body workout in 20 minutes or less - even in as few as four minutes - if you do what's known as TABATA training (20 seconds of hard exercise followed by 10 seconds of rest, repeated four times). The only caveat is ensuring technique isn't lost in the bid to retain intensity, because bad form leads to injury.

BENEFITS OF HIT

HIT is considered to be much more effective than a normal cardio session because the intensity is higher and you're able to increase both your aerobic and anaerobic endurance while burning more fat. HIT workouts are said to be fifty percent more efficient at burning blubber than low intensity exercise and have the additional benefit of firing up your metabolism so you continue torching calories long after you've finished your session - this is known as the afterburn. A recent study compared participants who did steady cardio for 30 minutes three times a week to those who did 20 minutes of high intensity interval training three times per week. Both groups showed similar weight loss, but the HIT group showed a two percent loss in body fat while the steady-cardio group lost only 0.3 percent. The HIT group also gained nearly two pounds of muscle, while the steady-state group lost almost a pound.

Key benefits include:

+ **Highly efficient fat burning**

+ **Increases the amount of oxygen your body can use which will raise your fitness level**

+ **Enables your body to process glucose better. The muscles utilise glucagon more readily, instead of storing it as fat**

+ **Builds lean muscle mass**

+ **Increases your energy levels and combats fatigue**

+ **Improves your quality of sleep**

HOW OFTEN SHOULD I BE DOING HIT?

In a proper high intensity training session, where you're going hell for leather, the central nervous system can take quite a pummeling. That's why we always recommend taking a minimum of 48 hours to recover. Overtraining can be as damaging as being sedentary, potentially causing raised cortisol levels, muscle damage, mechanical tension and metabolic stress. To counteract the strain you're putting your body under, always build in sufficient recovery time, make sure you eat well and sign up to regular deep tissue sports massages. Assuming you play by these rules, there's no reason HIIT can't be enjoyed two to three times a week.

ATHLETE LAB

110 CANNON STREET, THE CITY, EC4N 6EU

OPEN

MON-FRI.   6:00AM - 9:30PM
SAT.   8:00AM - 1:30PM
SUN.   CLOSED

🌐 ATHLETE-LAB.CO.UK

Ⓣ MONUMENT / BANK

At the heart of Cannon Street's corporate jungle sits Athlete Lab, a state-of-the-art indoor cycling studio that has hosted world-class riders like Laura Kenny and Ryan Mullen. Because the facility is equipped with real bikes (as opposed to indoor cycles), clients get the benefit of real power-based training. Whether your goal is to finish your first event, or to get an extra edge as a competitive cyclist, you can sign up for classes, one-on-one training, or head in to do your own session. Classes are open to all abilities, and all you need to remember is shorts and a top; towels, shoes and bottles are complimentary (and the trainers will fill up empty bottles mid-session to ensure you get the most out of your time). A large Race Board allows members to chalk their names under the races they are working towards, ideal for members looking to buddy-up. Such is the community that Athlete Lab have created, they now run team trips, bringing groups of members to races in the UK and Europe.

BOOM CYCLE

16 PROCTER STREET, HOLBORN, WC1V 6NX

OPEN

SEE WEBSITE FOR TIMETABLE

 BOOMCYCLE.CO.UK

 HOLBORN

With BOOM Cycle sessions regularly sold out in the busy BOOM venues, clearly Londoners can't get enough of this high-intensity, high-energy indoor cycling experience. The stairs that descend into the Holborn studio take you straight into the reception/waiting area. Here you're unlikely to miss the class before you emerge from the sultry darkness of the studio; high fives and sweaty smiles aside, the raw energy is visceral and infectious. This might be why the staff call themselves 'BOOM evangelists' - another indicator of the cult following amassed by BOOM. Once you've clipped in and you're ready to ride, whether at the front or the back, the staggered levels of the bikes gives everyone a clear view of the ultra-sassy instructor, leader of the BOOM brigade. Each 45-minute session is choreographed to a carefully curated playlist that varies depending on your instructor's favourite genre. We recommend checking ahead to get a session in your preferred style, so whether it's Kanye or Kygo you'll be inspired to keep in time to the beat. You'll be back before you know it, like a true BOOM-erang.

CYCLEBEAT

8 LOMBARD STREET, THE CITY, EC3V 9BJ

OPEN

MON-FRI.   6:30AM - 8:30PM
SAT-SUN.   CLOSED

🌐 CYCLEBEAT.CO.UK

Ⓔ MONUMENT

"Hey ho, let's go!" sprawls Cyclebeat's up tempo motto on a black wall in a dark room where 50 cycle bikes whizz. This indoor cycling venue attracts crowds from complete beginners to competitive cyclists, who enjoy the focused, hi-tech experience. A complimentary bike setup on registration ensures that you train in your optimum position and, crucially, avoid easily prevented injury. 'Beat Boards', reactive screens connected to the bikes and mounted on the front wall, help you track your performance and encourage competition - whether against yourself or another rider. You'll receive an email post-session with all of your statistics, meaning you can monitor your progression in the long term. The ultra dark studio makes for increased concentration, motivation and focus, and high energy music creates a buzzing atmosphere that will have you pedalling more ferociously than ever before. Each instructor has their own dedicated following based on coaching and music style, so groups are more like social and non-intimidating communities. With drinks, snacks and coconut water available at reception, Cyclebeat is a busy, high-energy fitness experience.

PSYCLE

CROSSRAIL PLACE, CANARY WHARF, E14 5LQ

When life gives you bikes, you've got to PSYCLE. That's what it comes down to at PSYCLE's Canary Wharf location. Though it's found on the downstairs level in the Crossrail Place, the studio is a modern glossy white which gives it a fresh sparkly feel. City slickers enter the changing rooms in suits and reappear as workout wonders. The upbeat music (free earplugs provided) and flashing disco lights make this the perfect after work escape - release your inner diva! For anyone that's never done an indoor cycling class before, PSYCLE is a baptism of fire. The steamed up mirrors at the front of the room lay testament to this. Expect to move from sitting to standing, doing arm presses and weights while the instructor tells you to remain grounded in yourself and who you are as a person. This mix of exercise and inspiration gives the enthusiastic 'PSYCLErs' what they came for, invigorated whoops and white towels lassoed over heads, means you've all made it through.

RIDE REPUBLIC

709 FULHAM ROAD, FULHAM, SW6 5UL

OPEN

MON-THU.	7:00AM - 9:00PM
FRI.	7:00AM - 7:30PM
SAT-SUN.	9:00AM - 4:00PM

RIDEREPUBLIC.CO.UK

PARSONS GREEN

This is one for the fast and the furious. Ride Republic is the place to come for a feisty competition with yourself and your class of hard-core riders. With a 'burn board' projected onto the front of the dimly-lit room, every session is an opportunity to smash your limits and your previous personal best. Ride Republic harnesses statistical technology attached to each bike to give you instant targets and objectives. The instructor tells you what resistance and power you should be on to keep the class working at a similar rate. This metrics-focused style of training means that you ride to win, the only thing you're there to lose is body fat. The pumping playlists keep your mind in gear but the what matters is your RMP and power output as opposed to your ability to stick in time with the beat. This suits those people that thrive on competition, adrenaline and endurance. Many of the regulars are in race training mode, though the occasional few just come to soak up the electric vibe of the ride. Ready, steady, ride.

HOW YOGA HAS GROWN AND STRETCHED

BY **JONATHAN SATTIN, FOUNDER + MANAGING DIRECTOR,** TRIYOGA

In 1984 when I first started practicing yoga, the choices of where to do it were limited. Either a one-to-one in a teacher's home, a church hall, or classes at The Iyengar Institute in Maida Vale or the Sivananda Ashram in Notting Hill. These two schools taught only their respective styles of yoga and that was it.

Much has changed since then and the phrase 'yoga industry' is often used to describe the culture of teaching yoga today in London.

From my perspective, between my first class in 1984 and 1997 (when I was putting together the plans for triyoga), not a lot had changed in the breadth and depth of the yoga industry in London – especially compared to the substantial growth in people's desire to keep fit and the number of health clubs. The first Holmes Place opened in 1980 and from then on, health clubs grew at an extraordinary rate. But yoga either was not part of their schedule or at the most it was nominal.

Meanwhile, in America the popularity of yoga was growing. In 1987 the first Yoga Works opened and whilst the original founders grew the number of centres to three by the time they sold the business in the early 2000's, it now has over 40. The original Yoga Works offered a broad range of styles, including Ashtanga Yoga, which was very different from most people's perception of yoga – the image we used to see most of the time was a woman seated in full lotus looking 'serene' – as Ashtanga was dynamic and strong. The U.S. yoga culture was then concentrated mainly on the east and west coasts.

In 1993 the Life Centre opened in Notting Hill and at that time it was known as more of an Ashtanga yoga centre. In the 1990s John Scott was teaching Mysore self-practice Ashtanga from the Royal Homeopathic Hospital in Queen's Square. Otherwise apart from these it was church halls and teachers' homes, or as we used to describe it, a bit brown rice and Birkenstocks. So, whilst there was some form of groundswell, what

happened to get us from there to where we are now?

By the time triyoga had its first building in 1999, there was also The Art of Health in Balham (which closed down a few years later) and Yoga Place in Bethnal Green Road. With this growing interest in yoga centres, the fitness industry was taking yoga more seriously, Third Space opened in Soho and The Laboratory in Muswell Hill – they both had more 'alternative' offerings. But, apart from them very few clubs offered anything other than a few classes.

When triyoga opened in Primrose Hill in 2000, we began a wave that helped carry the growing interest in yoga. Suddenly there was a large dedicated space that at its core wanted to make authentic yoga accessible to everyone. You didn't have to follow one style, you could find the best teachers and you could take time to find out what would really work for you. At the time, it was Europe's largest yoga studio and it broke the mould of what to expect.

I put the growth of yoga in London down to a growing awareness of Ashtanga yoga, celebrities like Madonna and Gwyneth Paltrow who publicised their yoga practice and general awareness that there are different and more conscious ways to look after ourselves.

Since then the yoga growth curve has been further driven by several factors, more teachers and better quality teaching, broader ranges of styles (some make me wonder), Bikram and other hot yoga centres and a stressful world in which we're trying to do more than just survive.

The underlying power of the practice will transform us no matter what.

BATTERSEA YOGA

2 KITE YARD, CAMBRIDGE ROAD, BATTERSEA, SW11 4TA

OPEN

MON-FRI.   7:00AM - 9:30PM

SAT-SUN.   8:00AM - 9:00PM

 BATTERSEAYOGA.COM

CLAPHAM JUNCTION

Right beside Battersea Park but tucked away down a gravelled drive, Battersea Yoga calls itself London's friendliest yoga studio. With a particular focus on mindfulness and meditation, you'll find two studios here - one large and lofty with an impressive gong as the centrepiece at the front, and the other a (much more intimate) converted garden shed. Purposefully, there are no mirrors in either studio as practise is about introspection, looking inside yourself not at yourself. The seclusion of Battersea Yoga transports you to a countryside retreat. The smaller studio is used mainly for one-to-one therapy, where sessions dealing with issues like stress, anxiety, emotional trauma or relationship problems take place. There is a focus on bioenergetics that listens to the disconnect between mind and body and aims to release both physical and psychological tensions. Breaking bad habits is a process, as is making new ones, so the courses here that run over a period of weeks are a good way to make and sustain positive changes.

BLUE COW YOGA

7 MOORGATE, THE CITY, EC2R 6AF

OPEN

MON–SUN   6:00AM – 9:00PM

 BLUECOWYOGA.CO.UK

 BANK / MOORGATE

Tucked away in a basement studio in Moorgate, Blue Cow Yoga offers city workers an oasis of tranquillity to escape to at any time of day. The atmosphere is friendly, welcoming and energising with a tangible buzz of activity. The entrance room provides a communal hub where members can enjoy free Wi-Fi, tea, coffee and fruit. Yoga and barre classes run throughout the day and vary in length and style. Morning classes are often gentler, helping Blue Cow yogis feel energised rather than exhausted before work. The

popular lunchtime session is a dynamic practise to help kick-start the afternoon ahead. Blue Cow Yoga brings two worlds together, providing hard-pressed Londoners the opportunity to experience the peace of the yogic tradition, right on their doorstep.

DOWN TO EARTH

129 FORTESS ROAD, TUFNELL PARK, NW5 2HR

OPEN

MON–FRI.   7:00AM – 10:00PM
SAT.   9:00AM – 6:00PM
SUN.   9:00AM – 9:00PM

 DOWNTOEARTHLONDON.
CO.UK

 TUFNELL PARK

Bright, fresh and beautifully designed, Down to Earth has a heavenly aesthetic. Green plants are dotted around reception and Down to Earth handmade pottery is for sale. The look is Scandinavian-inspired and the space is peaceful and uncluttered. The owner, Vanda Vucicevic, has created a blank canvas for people to 'bring their own story'. On the upper level there is one studio that floods with natural light and fits up to 16 people. They offer a spectrum of classes including: vinyasa flow, restorative, iyengar, yin, pregnancy, hatha, and kids yoga,

as well as Pilates and occasional weekend workshops. There is also one treatment room.

FIERCE GRACE

200 REGENT'S PARK ROAD, CHALK FARM, NW1 8BE

OPEN

MON-SUN.   7:00AM - 9:30PM

 FIERCEGRACE.COM

 CHALK FARM

Buzzing is the only word that can pinpoint the atmosphere at Fierce Grace Hot Yoga in Primrose Hill. One of six Fierce Grace studios, legions of class goers swing through the door to check in and pick up mats, towels and two-litre bottles of water before filing into the steamy class. They'll need it; Michele Pernetta, founder of the company, pioneered Bikram (hot) Yoga in the UK, so if anyone knows what they are doing, it's her. It's no frills here, and that works. Instead of a competitive atmosphere, you'll find a genuine community of a variety of people, from beginners to advanced, men and women. The signature class 'Fierce Grace' is a 90-minute 100% body workout for all levels, which is performed to music. The method combines Hatha, Power and Ashtanga yoga, as well as interval and core training, channelling deep expression of the self. You'll leave feeling strong, graceful, toned and really very sweaty. Good thing there are showers, products and refuel snacks and drinks available. For a total escape, book onto a Fierce Grace retreat in India, Italy or Turkey; there, you will progress through six days of yoga activity, and leave city limits behind with sun, food, wine and brilliant company.

HOTPOD YOGA

9 - 15 HELMSLEY PLACE, HACKNEY, E8 3SB

OPEN

SEE WEBSITE FOR TIMETABLE

 HOTPODYOGA.COM

 LONDON FIELDS

Come to the very place that HotPod Yoga was born to experience the root beginnings of this increasingly popular franchise brand. Close to London Fields, in a large red-brick warehouse and up some unassuming black metal stairs, the hot pod is all blown up and ready for flow. What initially appears to be a big purple bouncy castle is actually an inflatable heated studio. Able to fit up to 24 people, the idea behind this concept is to create an immersive and nurturing space that remains consistently the same every time you practice. The pods are portable in their design in order to make hot yoga and its benefits accessible to all. Step inside and it's easy to forget the workings and worries of the outside world. Dimly lit with coloured lighting, there are no mirrors inside the pod. The heat and humidity in this bubble-like structure creates a calming ambience that is further complimented by the music chosen to accompany the sequence of moves. For post-yoga purposes: there is only one shower and you must bring your own towels.

INDABA YOGA STUDIO

18 HAYES PLACE, MARYLEBONE, NW1 6UA

OPEN

MON-FRI.   6:30AM - 9:00PM

SAT-SUN.   8:30AM - 7:00PM

 INDABAYOGA.COM

 MARYLEBONE

Conveniently close to Marylebone station, Indaba Yoga Studio is an extremely popular spot for yogis looking to perfect their poses. With a range of classes, treatments and workshops; the environment here is focused upon the importance of learning, developing and evolving, both in yourself and your practice. Indaba is a great choice of studio for anyone new to yoga, their range of beginner classes and welcoming atmosphere make it easy to appreciate the many benefits of this mindful art. Every teacher here has their own

distinctive style of teaching, we recommend experimenting with what appeals to you. Whether it's acro yoga, hot yoga or even the dharma yoga master class, your strength and flexibility will improve as much as your attendance is valued.

IYENGAR YOGA INSTITUTE

223A RANDOLPH AVENUE, MAIDA VALE, W9 1NL

OPEN

M, T + THU.   9:00AM - 8:30PM

WED.   8:00AM - 8:30PM

FRI.   9:00AM - 7:00PM

SAT.   8:00AM - 5:30PM

SUN.   9:00AM - 6:30PM

 IYI.ORG.UK

 MAIDA VALE

Tucked away down a small path in Maida Vale, Iyengar Yoga Institute is a neighbourhood treasure, one that's been welcoming new students and experienced practitioners for more than 30 years. The venue is flooded with natural light, your healthy dose of Vitamin D. There are two studios in which classes of varied skill levels take place. For those that are serious about Iyengar, teacher training programmes are also on offer. With plants lining the walls and huge skylights throughout, this

space can only be described as serene. On a nice day, enjoy a breath of fresh air in the beautiful courtyard after class - a peaceful spot to relax and reflect.

THE LIFE CENTRE

15 EDGE STREET, NOTTING HILL, W8 7PN

OPEN

MON–FRI.   7:15AM – 9:30PM

SAT.   8:30AM – 7:00PM

SUN.   8:30AM – 7:30PM

 THELIFECENTRE.COM

 NOTTING HILL GATE

From Bayswater road, or Ladbroke Grove, a short, meandering walk, through streets endowed with candy coloured houses you find in Notting Hill, takes you to The Life Centre. This yoga and Pilates studio is about lifelong wellbeing. The centre specialises in pregnancy, mums and babies classes; promising to guide attendees through the special, but often daunting time around childbirth. Other classes span from forest yoga and aerial yoga, to yoga for teens and kids, to jivamukti spiritual warrior.

Retreats, too, are available to book onto via teachers at The Life Centre. These range from Norfolk, to South India and beyond, aiming to enrich people with the means to fully come home to their bodies.

LUMI POWER YOGA

121 KING STREET, HAMMERSMITH, W6 9JG

OPEN

MON–THU.   6:00AM – 9:00PM

FRI.   6:00AM – 8:00PM

SAT.   8:00AM – 6:15PM

SUN.   8:00AM – 8:00PM

 LUMIPOWERYOGA.COM

 HAMMERSMITH

A popular destination through word of mouth, the King Street entrance to Lumi Power Yoga makes it an unassuming find. Once upstairs, classes take place in one of their two sizeable studios either 'Roots' or 'Wings' on the floor above. Both rooms have pleasantly large windows that give the yogi sun salute renewed meaning. At its busiest on Saturday mornings, Lumi hustles and bustles with positive energy and self-expression. The Lumi Power-Hot class with Elina Iso-Rautio at 10am is their signature class which combines breath and movement into a fluid sequence. Taught

in a heated studio, a little extra dynamism infuses the flow of the class, a great one to stretch and strengthen the body and the mind.

THE POWER YOGA COMPANY

11 - 12 LETTICE STREET, FULHAM, SW6 4EH

OPEN

MON-FRI.   6:30AM - 9:30PM

SAT-SUN.   8:00AM - 7:45PM

 THEPOWERYOGACO.COM

 PARSONS GREEN

As its name suggests, this studio is London's first to specialise in Power Yoga, a dynamic version of vinyasa flow based on the ashtanga series. Yin, flow and restore and kid's yoga are also on offer, with levels ranging from complete beginner to advanced. Here, your body is really cared for; with postnatal yoga and yoga for those living with cancer, The Power Yoga Company has established itself as a place of refuge and recovery. The upstairs reception area is flooded with natural light thanks to a large window; incense and candles burn on the large table and the clean white glow for the walls is set off with wood rafters high in the lofty ceiling.

SANGYÉ YOGA

300 KENSAL ROAD, LADBROKE GROVE, W10 5BE

OPEN

MON-FRI.   7:00AM - 9:00PM

SAT-SUN.   9:00AM - 6:30PM

 SANGYEYOGA.COM

 WESTBOURNE PARK / LADBROKE GROVE

One floor up in a Kensal office building, this studio is an unexpected, peaceful sanctuary. Sangyé Yoga School is a Jivamukti Affiliate; community-focused, the school welcomes most of its class-goers from the Kensal and Notting Hill areas and exudes a friendly atmosphere. The School provides a space where independent Jivamukti Yoga teachers can host classes or workshops. With more than 50 classes each week, from Spiritual Warrior with Huma Jalil of the Himalayan foothills of Pakistan, to Vinyasa with Cat, Sangyé offers classes suitable for every level of yoga practitioner. The two studio rooms share a foldable wall, which gets pushed back for big events; mostly when a well-known guest teacher holds the class. With the canal side just around the corner, this is an ideal spot to reconnect physically, philosophically and spiritually.

STUDIO ONE ISLINGTON

237 CALEDONIAN ROAD, ISLINGTON, N1 1ED

OPEN
SEE WEBSITE FOR TIMETABLE

 STUDIOONE.CO

 KING'S CROSS

Touch your toes before you've had time to touch your toast at Studio One's early morning Dynamic Yoga class. Situated between Islington and King's Cross, this boutique studio and its whitewashed walls, is the epitome of wellness. In addition to yoga they also offer: Reformer Pilates, Barre, Boxing and Pre & Post-Natal classes. The downstairs studio has a movable wall that can split the large room in two which means the number of people in the classes can vary from 2 to 20. Try their signature Method class which combines dance cardio, boxing, yoga and Pilates to fuse HIIT and mindfulness. This is especially good for those that want to tone and strengthen both the body and the mind.

TOTAL CHI

243 BAKER STREET, MARYLEBONE, NW1 6XE

OPEN
SEE WEBSITE FOR TIMETABLE

 TOTALCHI.COM

 BAKER STREET

This stunning white space is a total sanctuary, especially in contrast to the disgruntled queues for The Sherlock Holmes Museum, bulging out onto Baker Street. At Total Chi Yoga Bar, every element has been carefully considered. This top-of-the-range yoga centre boasts two studio rooms, luxury changing facilities and an impressive refuel and coffee bar. This means that everything you could possibly need is on hand - down to own brand water, towels and non-slip mats for hot yoga. From the moment you enter, the place sparkles; it's so obviously squeaky clean and cared for, and makes for a relaxed start. The downstairs studios are small, with heating functions (hot yoga is performed at up to 32 degrees) and colourful mood lighting. Huge windows in the larger studio look straight onto a tranquil garden of green plants, a water feature and a buddha. Classes here are of no more than six, which gives them a very personal feel. Students are called by name and the space is yours to experiment in. Dreamy.

OPEN

SEE WEBSITE FOR TIMETABLE

 TRIYOGA.CO.UK

 FULHAM BROADWAY

TRIYOGA

372 KING'S ROAD, CHELSEA, SW3 5UZ

With four studios in the heart of London (Soho, Camden, Chelsea and Covent Garden), triyoga are legends in the London yogasphere. They offer classes, workshops and regular courses in yoga, meditation, Pilates and barre. They also offer a number of treatments to keep your mind and body in balance and prevent injury from frequent practice. Their Chelsea location has 3 beautiful studios that light up like the heavens with the gloriously large windows. The presence of natural light during the day, especially for those early starts, gives a rejuvenating feel to the flow. One of the three is a far infrared heated studio, which is where the signature 'triyoga hot' classes take place. This far infrared heats the body as opposed to the air, allowing you to bend into a deeper, more intensive stretches. With slick changing rooms, disabled access, an organic café and juice bar, as well as a yoga and lifestyle shop, this place is well worth a tri.

UNION STATION YOGA

18 LAVENDER HILL, BATTERSEA, SW11 5RW

OPEN

MON-THU.   6:45AM - 9:15PM

FRI.   6:45AM - 8:00PM

SAT-SUN.   8:45AM - 7:45PM

 UNIONSTATIONYOGA.CO.UK

 CLAPHAM COMMON

Lavender Hill residents are lucky to have Union Station Yoga on their doorstep. This charming yoga studio has a community feel that welcomes students of all ages and abilities through its glassy doors. The classes range from gentle hatha and yin, to power and flow. The owner, Paula Le Dao, hails from Vancouver and has brought that west coast positivity across the Atlantic with her. As you walk through the door there's a comfortable looking sofa and a shoes-off policy to abide by.

The studio itself is a comfortable size, with small classes, it allows the practise to feel personal. Don't expect any high fives here, you're more likely to get a hug and a warm cup of herbal tea after class!

THE WELL GARDEN

HACKNEY DOWNS STUDIOS, 17 AMHURST TERRACE, HACKNEY, E8 2BT

OPEN

MON-SUN.   7:00AM - 9:30PM

 THEWELLGARDEN.CO.UK

RECTORY ROAD RAIL

While it might sound cliché, The Well Garden is one of East London's best kept secrets. Found within Hackney Downs studios and right next to Hackney Downs park, this rustic hub of wellbeing offers yoga, gong meditation, and a whole range of alternative treatments. The therapists and teachers differ in their styles but share in their attention to detail and impactful practice. There are 3 treatment rooms and the yoga studio fits around 21 people with up to 7 classes per day. This rustic spot is the opposite of a highly commercialised central London space - it suits those

that want an authentic and community-focused feel. The reception is adorned with green plants and wicker chairs to put you in a peaceful frame of mind and the general crowd is mainly regulars and locals. Namaste.

YOGA WEST

33 - 34 WESTPOINT, WARPLE WAY, ACTON, W3 0RG

OPEN

MON-FRI.   6:30AM - 9:30PM

SAT-SUN.   8:00AM - 8:00PM

 YOGAAT.COM

TURNHAM GREEN /
ACTON CENTRAL

Yoga West (private yoga and Pilates provider) is YogaAt's first brick and mortar studio. Located in residential West London, the studio caters largely for residents of the Shepherd's Bush, Acton and Chiswick areas. Accessibility is the ethos here - everyone is treated equally, whether they are 20 years into yoga practice, or have only just discovered that vinyasa flow doesn't refer to the mouth of a river. At Yoga West instructors will remember your name, and class-goers socialise together; with Pollen + Grace salads available, what better excuse to relax and have a chinwag? Early morning ashtanga yoga is popular - an ideal method to wake your body up with a boost. Yoga West offers a wide range of specialised classes, like jivamukti, Pilates mat class, parent and baby yoga and pregnancy yoga. These pre and postnatal classes are a specialty of this studio, helping participants adapt to their changing bodies, and prepare mentally and physically for childbirth. Additionally, the studio runs workshops, including a 6 week yoga foundation course. No matter why you are there, large windows flood the white studio with light, creating the perfect setting to connect mind and body.

YOGAHAVEN

26 KEW ROAD, KEW GARDENS, TW9 2NA

OPEN

MON-SUN.   6:30AM - 10:00PM

 YOGAHAVEN.CO.UK

 RICHMOND

"It's always impossible until it's done," scrolls black writing across the Yogahaven Richmond studio wall - just in case your concentration slips out of focus during class. Specialising in 'leela', a unique form of hot yoga, classes here are suitable for everyone. The sweat will pour, but you'll leave each class feeling in balance and stronger, mentally and physically. From Hot Yoga Basics to Hot Flow and Hot Yoga Fusion, the studio's specialty is clear; the room temperature gets hiked up to 36 degrees for an intense atmosphere. If heat isn't for you then try out one of Yogahaven's non-heated classes, like jivamukti, rocket yoga or vinyasa flow. The popular Candlelit Yin & Yang class is a great way to unwind, find balance and reset. Yogahaven also have London venues in Clapham and Islington.

YOTOPIA

13 MERCER STREET, COVENT GARDEN, WC2H 9QJ

OPEN

MON-FRI.   6:30AM - 9:00PM
SAT.   9:00AM - 7:00PM
SUN.   8:30AM - 7:30PM

 YOTOPIA.CO.UK

 LEICESTER SQUARE /
       COVENT GARDEN

With over 20 top London yoga teachers, this peaceful escape in the heart of Covent Garden offers every class that a budding yogi could wish for. Step inside and find yourself in an oasis of calm - the simplicity and muted colours will settle and focus the mind. Expect a friendly welcome and helpful advice about classes and what will suit you, whether you're brand new to this ancient art or already practising your inversions. Yotopia offers two studios, one with a state-of-the-art heating and humidification system, where 'hot' classes are taught at around 36°C. Both studios are spacious, minimal and mirror free - students

are encouraged to focus on their internal journey and gain a deeper understanding of each posture.

YOGA

BY **AYA ETHERINGTON, PERSONAL TRAINER + YOGA INSTRUCTOR,** EQUINOX KENSINGTON

London is a fast-paced and vibrant place where people work hard and long hours. As businesses become more international and diverse, much of the day is spent sat at a desk and in front of a computer, and leisure time is increasingly spent on social media, and on our phones. We have not yet discovered what toll this will take on both the body and the mind in the long term.

As our bodies get used to sitting in chairs, being still for hours on end, maybe with an occasional lunch or coffee break consisting of fast and convenient foods, alongside long and stressful commuting hours this will inevitably lead to increased stress levels, weakened muscles and a visible difference in posture standing or sitting.

The increasing reliance on screen technology for both personal and professional routine, limited access to natural light, fresh air and green spaces, will mean vitamin deficiencies which can translate to poor gut health and mental wellbeing.

Over the past ten years in London there has been a steady increase in people practicing yoga with new studios and pop-up classes held all over the city as even the tiniest of places can be utilised as yoga or meditation spaces. Doing yoga can help bring stillness and calm to the mind and with regular practice, strength and flexibility to our bodies by flowing through a sequence of moves that are otherwise not used anymore in day-to-day life. Yoga is an ancient practice that provides a varying workout. It needs nothing more than our bodies and a mat to increase our heart rate in a very natural way which is accessible to all fitness and age groups.

The beauty of yoga is that it can be tailored to suit your day-to-day needs. Contrary to popular belief, a session does not have to be limited to a certain length of time or effort level. Anyone can reap the benefits that regular yoga sessions can bring to day to day living.

If you feel energetic you can do a fast paced and challenging flow. If you need to calm down choose a style more grounded. Every class is designed to help release stress and detox. The body sweats which releases endorphins (the happy hormones) and then a series of challenging balances help move the body into twists. These squeeze toxins out of your organs and lengthens muscles to gently increase flexibility finishing with quiet and relaxed breathing to end peacefully and gain distance from your worries and negative energy.

At the end of each traditional class, you are encouraged to empty your mind and allow a brief 5 minute interval to separate day-to-day mental stresses in order to gain distance and perspective allowing you to "wake-up" with a peaceful and calm attitude. If nothing else, the 5 minute electronic detox allows the space to tune in with what you might need from your day, not just what your boss, friends or family need from you. In the fast life of London, it is important to try and protect yourself from overcommitting both socially and professionally to avoid mentally and physically burning out.

The practice of clearing the mind after every class allows you to re-approach the problems and stress that plagued your mind from a fresh and clean angle. This is especially key in a fast-paced, dynamic environment where the natural business of the city can quickly translate into a frantic mental challenge by teaching the ability to 'keep calm and carry on', rather than get swept up in whirlwind.

Techniques learnt by practicing yoga, such as stilling the mind and breath, can be enforced for a minute during a stressful day, (right in the office by sitting up straight at your desk, or standing in a toilet cubicle)

to re-engage with that reset button feeling that you get after a class.

Of course, London has many distractions and exciting things to do but once you practice yoga, you feel like you have pushed reset button, you sleep well, and when looking after your physical body, this in time will also make you respect yourself, and want to also practice the art of eating well. A lifestyle that encourages the art of self-worth and self-respect will ensure that you gain confidence that will translate positively in relationships both professionally and personally.

The physical results of practicing yoga are increased flexibility, increase in strength, awareness of your body and getting to move in a way that you didn't think possible.

One of the subtler benefits is both tuning into and out of our turbulent thoughts. In each yoga session you should take the chance to ask yourself: how do I feel? You become more conscious of your physical wellbeing and your thoughts as they rush back to you at the end of practice, and this can help highlight what is causing discomfort and stress in your life. Even if the practice is only a 10 minute sequence at the beginning or the end of the day using an app, or a YouTube tutorial, it will help soothe the body and mind in order to tackle the hectic lifestyle of city living.

The Equinox yoga studio is a place to shut out the world, get centered and deepen your practice. Classes include Power Yoga and Dynamic Vinyasa Yoga.

equinox.com

Seated Twist

Warrior II

Upward Dog

ABSOLUTE PILATES

UNIT G, 19 HEATHMAN'S ROAD, FULHAM, SW6 4TJ

OPEN

MON-SUN.   7:00AM - 8:00PM

 ABSOLUTEPILATESPLUS.COM

 PARSONS GREEN

Located on Parsons Green's eclectic fitness haven, Heathman's Road, this Pilates studio couldn't be more in-keeping with its surroundings. Occupying a super white loft style space, it feels distinctly New York; an upmarket, focused experience for your body. The reception area is small but comfortable, with a spread of luxury lifestyle magazines on the coffee table, and a refuel bar should you need an extra boost. Upstairs is the main studio space - accessible by a spiral staircase - where Dynamic Reformer Pilates (Absolute Pilates' specialty) is held. Dynamic Reformer Pilates, available one-on-one or as a timetabled class, is a machine based workout, targeting muscle groups and working them to their core, leading, over time, to a sculpted, lean physique, complete with increased calorie burn. The light, well-equipped space is a motivational area devoid of distraction. HIIT classes are also offered, mainly in the evenings in the two smaller downstairs studios. The changing rooms are fitted with showers, hair tools and some toiletries, so that you can rush straight off to work - or for dinner - feeling fresh and revitalised.

BEPILATES

78A CHILTERN STREET, MARYLEBONE, W1U 5AB

OPEN
BY APPOINTMENT

 BE-PILATES.CO.UK

 BAKER STREET

bePilates is one of the most sought after and highly-specialised Pilates studios in London. Situated in prime Marylebone position on Chiltern Street, the studio is locked from the outside and you must book in advance if you would like an appointment. In January 2017, the class structure changed to adopt a more personalised, holistic-yet-targeted approach. bePilates is endowed with every piece of equipment under the sun from the Pilates repertoire. This specialised space requires every new member to complete three private introduction sessions before joining group classes, to become well acquainted with the equipment and thereby maximise core results.

BOOTCAMP PILATES

64 PORCHESTER ROAD, BAYSWATER, W2 6ET

OPEN
SEE WEBSITE FOR TIMETABLE

 BOOTCAMPPILATES.COM

 ROYAL OAK

Bootcamp Pilates claims to have transformed the Reformer Pilates market with state-of-the-art equipment, elite trainers and a diverse class timetable. Here, you can enjoy a wide range of sessions, from Pilates, to HIIT and cardio Pilates to Motor Body Blitz. Standard reformer Pilates is most popular at this studio. With a variety of over 250 movements, the class tests flexibility, coordination and balance, promoting fitness and strength with dynamic movements. The studio is bright and welcoming, ideal for anybody looking to better understand their body, becoming stronger and more flexible in the process. Bend it like Bootcamp Pilates!

CORE KENSINGTON

64 PORCHESTER ROAD, BAYSWATER, W2 6ET

OPEN

MON-THU.	6:30AM - 9:00PM
FRI.	6:30AM - 5:00PM
SAT.	9:00AM - 3:00PM
SUN.	9:00AM - 2:30PM

 COREKENSINGTON.CO.UK

 ROYAL OAK

The Core Kensington studio can be found on the lower ground floor of the Bootcamp Pilates Nottinghill. Wonderfully close to Royal Oak tube station, this is an easy spot to try out if you regularly whizz past on the circle line. The reformer Pilates classes are taught in the STOTT® method - a contemporary, anatomically-based approach to Joseph Pilates' original exercise method. This contemporary take on the classical Pilates repertoire acknowledges the natural curvature of the spine and includes techniques from physiotherapy to aid successful rehabilitation. Especially good for anyone with spinal problems, the Core Kensington team welcome all ages and abilities. The exercises strengthen core muscles which results in superior spinal stability and injury prevention. The aim is to make you strong, not bulky. Classes are kept small, with a maximum of 5 people so corrections and modifications can easily be made. With specially designed Pilates gear and equipment, you'll work on fluidity and breathing, as well as control of the body with your mind. Come here to keep in line.

FORM W11

77A LONSDALE ROAD, NOTTING HILL, W11 2DF

OPEN

MON-THU.	6:30AM - 8:30PM
FRI.	6:30AM - 8:00PM
SAT.	9:00AM - 6:00PM
SUN.	9:00AM - 8:30PM

 FORMSTUDIOS.CO.UK

 LADBROKE GROVE

Form W11 couldn't be closer to the hustle and bustle of Portobello Market, and in some ways, it's a reflection of its neighbourhood. The small corridor which leads to class buzzes with Pilates lovers, chatting on the bench outside the studio space. Founder Elissa El Hadj wanted to go against the grain of packed out Pilates classes by limiting the size of the group to just 8 people per class. Established as a studio that would focus specifically on form, here, attention is on technique. It also claims to be the first London studio to introduce MOTR, a foam

roller-like piece of equipment with extendable arms, used to perform a blend of Pilates, TRX and barre. METcore is the signature workout here, involving Pilates and metabolic conditioning in a 50-minute full body workout.

HEARTCORE

26A QUEEN'S TERRACE, ST JOHN'S WOOD, NW8 6EA

OPEN

MON-FRI.	6:15AM - 8:30PM
SAT.	8:30AM - 2:30PM
SUN.	8:30AM - 7:00PM

 HEARTCORE.CO.UK

 ST JOHN'S WOOD

Located in a converted church one minute from St John's Wood station, the best feature of Heartcore is arguably the main studio area itself, on the upper floor of the premise. It's a large space, flooded with light from the majestic church window; with sheet white walls and mirrors to boot, the brightness is dazzlingly beautiful. If there were a fitness nirvana, this would be it. Heartcore offers classes spanning from reformer Pilates, full, upper and lower body TRX, and Barre. The ethos, as set out by founder Jess Schuring, is

'anything but average'. It's a passionate, finely tuned arena for high quality workouts, and you'll leave feeling fitter and better both physically and mentally.

PHIIT LONDON

345 NORTH END ROAD, FULHAM, SW6 1NN

OPEN

MON-FRI.	6:00AM - 8:15PM
SAT.	8:00AM - 4:00PM
SUN.	9:00AM - 4:00PM

 PHIIT.CO.UK

WEST BROMPTON /
FULHAM BROADWAY

A clever acronym, PHIIT stands for Pilates High-Intensity Interval Training and that's exactly what you'll get. This studio is well hidden, and certainly one of those places you're unlikely to come across unless you've heard about it. Located on Fulham's North End road, PHIIT is in the basement of the Shopping Palace. With one studio, the group classes are kept small and intimate in order to give enough individual attention to each person. Their 3 signature classes range between PHIIT Pilates, PHIIT Killer and PHIIT Hybrid, the diversity of which helps to build cardiovascular fitness as well as core body strength. It's recommended that you mix up your workout schedule to incorporate the different classes over the course of the week, so you constantly feel challenged and inspired. Personal training and nutritional coaching are available to book for those on a real health kick. Here, the instructors want to keep you PHIIT for life - it's survival of the fittest after all...

OPEN

MON-THU.	7:00AM - 9:15PM
FRI.	7:00AM - 8:15PM
SAT.	9:00AM - 3:00PM
SUN.	9:00AM - 4:00PM

 TEN.CO.UK

 GREEN PARK

TEN HEALTH AND FITNESS

6 DUKE STREET, MAYFAIR, SW1Y 6BN

With six studios across central London, Ten Health and Fitness offer a combination of dynamic Pilates, pre/post-natal training, personal training, HIIT, barre, physiotherapy and sports massage. Upon your first visit, you'll be warmly welcomed into what they refer to as 'the circle of care'. The Duke Street entrance will lead you downstairs to their St James' studio, best visited for their hard-core advanced dynamic Reformer Pilates classes. These step up the pace and intensity of the movements and offer a varied and demanding workout that incorporates more functional progressions. The emphasis here is on both effort and result. There is a maximum of 10 people per reformer Pilates and barre classes, and for TRX and HIIT the limit is 5 - which means there's no escape for the slackers. Certainly one for both men and women, this form of exercise helps to strengthen, tighten and tone as well as improve bad posture from slouching at a desk. There are showers, free towels and beauty products to make sure that you leave looking ten out of ten.

VITA PILATES

1A IVES STREET, CHELSEA, SW3 2ND

OPEN

MON-FRI.	6:30AM - 9:30PM
SAT.	8:30AM - 5:30PM
SUN.	9:30AM - 5:30PM

 VITA-PILATES.COM

 SOUTH KENSINGTON

While Vita Pilates is only a 7 minute walk from South Kensington tube, this studio is the furthest you can get from the latest boutique fitness gym/nightclub fusion. Better suited to those that relish small, intimate classes, Vita Pilates offers a combination of Dynamic Reformer and barre Pilates. With a maximum of 8 people per class, it is also possible to book one-on-one personal instruction. Whether you're 16 or 60, this type of workout is good for the whole body and will stretch and strengthen muscles you previously didn't know existed. Attracting an international clientele, as well as local residents from the surrounding area, it's possible to buy membership, small package deals, or spontaneously drop in for a one-off class.
There is a small shop downstairs should you be keen to update your athleisure look, as well as smart mahogany wood changing rooms with showers, hair-dryers and freshly pressed towels. Live La dolce vita!

BARRECORE

18 KENSINGTON CHURCH STREET, KENSINGTON, W8 4PT

OPEN

SEE WEBSITE FOR TIMETABLE

 BARRECORE.CO.UK

 KENSINGTON HIGH STREET

In London, Barrecore now has locations in Wimbledon, Chelsea, Chiswick, Kensington, Hampstead and Mayfair (with more to come). This barre fitness concept is clearly a hit with Londoners from every area. The ballet-based classes are designed for all ages and abilities, and aim to get you feeling strong and sculpted, with the physique of a dancer. The signature class uses your own bodyweight, lightweight props and high repetitions - you'll be surprised at how such small isometric movements can be such hard work. The main focus is on the arms, thighs, seat and core, those classic wobbly areas we tend to keep covered up! Just off Kensington High Street, the venue can be found downstairs and has one main studio and a personal training studio with showers, lockers and free towels provided. As well as the signature, stretch and sculpt classes that last 55 minutes, Barrecore also offer HIIT and cardio sessions to get the heart rate up. You'll find yourself pirouetting out of the studio and straight into a warm bath to relax those hard-worked muscles.

BARRETONED

12 CHEPSTOW ROAD, NOTTING HILL, W2 5BD

OPEN

MON-FRI.	7:00AM - 8:15PM
SAT.	8:30AM - 1:15PM
SUN.	9:45AM - 2:00PM

 BARRETONED.COM

 NOTTING HILL

'The shake' is top priority at this bright, friendly barre studio just off ever-buzzing Westbourne Grove. The BARREtoned classic 60-minute high intensity, low impact workout targets specific muscle groups so powerfully with sequences of repeated movements that your muscles will burn and shake (this is good). BARREtoned Express is all the rage; the 12.30pm 45-minute class is a compressed barre workout designed to fit neatly into your lunch break. You won't be dripping pools of

sweat, but you will feel instantly stronger, stretchier and more elongated. 'Once you go barre, you'll never go back,' is the house motto, and it's easy to see why.

DANCEWORKS STUDIOS

16 BALDERTON STREET, MAYFAIR, W1K 6TN

OPEN

MON-FRI.	8:00AM - 10:00PM
SAT-SUN.	9:00AM - 6:00PM

 DANCEWORKS.NET

 BOND STREET

Danceworks offers drop-in classes for everyone, every day. Whether you're looking to learn a new groove, swing through the salsa or take a chance with the cha-cha-cha, there's something to suit. With 6 studios and a mixed offering of Ballet, World Dance, Street/Commercial, Contemporary/Jazz, Tap, Pilates and Barre as well as Martial Arts, it's the perfect place to try out an exciting new style. With over 20 classes on every day, Danceworks has a friendly and inclusive vibe that makes it easy to let your hair loose and bounce to the beat. During the day classes tend to be geared

toward intermediate/professional levels, but a more general standard is catered for in the evening. On the first floor, you'll find a Natureworks wellbeing area that offers complementary therapies to help with dance and sports related injuries. Ready for your West End debut?

PAOLA'S BODYBARRE

55A HIGH STREET, WIMBLEDON VILLAGE, WIMBLEDON, SW19 5BA

OPEN

MON-FRI.   6:45AM - 9:00PM

SAT-SUN.   8:00AM - 12:00PM

🌐 PAOLASBODYBARRE.COM

⊖ WIMBLEDON

Barre classes with Paola Di Lanzo are fierce, focused and leave you feeling amazing about what your body can do. Based in 10 sites around London, with over 30 trainers, Paola's Body Barre is known as one of the best in the business. The Wimbledon studio became Paola's home site in 2017, along with plans for expansion in Chelsea. Having been a fitness professional since the 80s, Paola was inspired by small, boutique studios, which went against the grain of the super gyms that were so fashionable at the time. In recent years, she quickly cottoned on to millennials, who prefer to indulge in brunch and green juice post-Pilates, rather than party. Since opening her doors as Paola's Body Barre in Fulham in 2014, she has carved out a hardcore-chic business model where results speak for themselves. Her workouts are designed to have optimum effect in minimal time; if you want to lift your bottom that little bit more, Paola will make it happen. Her class format is upping the London anti, it includes more reps on the barre, more cardio, and dynamic Pilates. Giving high profile talks and sessions at venues including Soho Farmhouse, Paola is the ultimate London barre guru.

PINEAPPLE DANCE STUDIOS

LONDON OPERA HOUSE, 7 LANGLEY STREET, COVENT GARDEN, WC2H 9JA

OPEN

MON-FRI.	8:30AM - 10:00PM
SAT.	9:00AM - 7:00PM
SUN.	10:00AM - 6:00PM

 PINEAPPLE.UK.COM

 COVENT GARDEN

The Pineapple brand is so famous that it's likely a household name for many. Initially established by Debbie Moore in a disused pineapple warehouse, this dance venue has evolved beyond measure, now with 10 studios in its home on Langley Street. It looks every bit 'dance school', towering up over five floors, where the corridors echo with excited chatter, footfall and studio music, but it's not exclusive in the slightest. Here, beginner classes are taught by the exact same teacher that takes the professional level class; meaning constantly

high attention to detail and the ability to progress through levels at your own pace with the same teacher. With over 250 weekly classes and 20 styles of dance - from jazz and ballet to Bollywood Fusion - this is a buzzing urban dance hotspot.

SEEN ON SCREEN

CENTRAL YMCA CLUB, 112 GREAT RUSSELL STREET, FITZROVIA, WC1B 3NQ

OPEN

SEE WEBSITE FOR TIMETABLE

 SEENONSCREENFITNESS.COM

 TOTTENHAM COURT ROAD

Think you can't dance like Beyoncé? Think again. Seen on Screen (SoS) have pioneered a fitness trend that teaches women how to strut their stuff like their favourite pop icons. With classes taking place in gyms across London, these fun, friendly workouts are spreading fast. SoS's main studio at the Central YMCA Club offers a diverse range of classes that change weekly, from 'Drop it Like a Squat' and 'Hip Hop Movie Masterclass' to 'Sweat', 'De-stress' and many more. Instructors are regularly 'seen on screen' having danced with global names, including Beyoncé,

Rihanna, Christina Aguilera and Little Mix - but that doesn't mean you need experience to join in; beginners are welcome.

FITNESS DANCE + BARRECORE

XTEND BARRE

49 MARYLEBONE HIGH STREET, MARYLEBONE, W1U 5HH

OPEN

MON-FRI.   6:00AM - 9:00PM

SAT.   9:30AM - 3:30PM

SUN.   9:30AM - 6:00PM

XTENDBARRE.COM

BAKER STREET /
BOND STREET

This beautifully conceived barre studio fits right into its surroundings in the heart of upmarket Marylebone. A large white space with light wooden floors welcomes you. Xtend Barre is quite different from other barre studios across the capital; here, each class is more movement-focused, cardio-intensive and incorporates a larger proportion of dance moves. The concept leaves no room for breaks. You keep going, but within every set, there is one slightly easier move, acting as active recovery. Classes are generally composed of four sections - warm up, glutes, abs and upper body - like mini workouts in themselves, each section ends with stretching out. At Xtend Barre, the instructors have a dance background (they teach ballet too), and are invariably positive, bouncing around providing encouragement in those moments where the shake is so intense you risk giving in. This support pushes you harder and the benefits are instantly noticeable; you'll feel lifted and toned up. A community has quickly and assuredly formed around this studio. Case in point, the 60-day 'make a positive change' challenge they launched had so many sign ups that they had to invest in a second large wall chart to fit everyone's names on.

BXR LONDON

24 PADDINGTON STREET, MARYLEBONE, W1U 5QX

OPEN

MON-FRI.	6:30AM - 9:30PM
SAT.	8:00AM - 8:00PM
SUN.	8:00AM - 6:00PM

🌐 BXRLONDON.COM

🚇 BAKER STREET

Carefully crafted and beautifully designed, at BXR London not a kettlebell is out of place. Competitors will have to seriously step up their game to avoid being knocked out of the ring. A clever combination of the old-school membership model with the newer boutique fitness drop-in classes, this gym offers both, it really hits the spot. The ground floor is where SWEAT by BXR takes place. With 3 concept studios: Technique, Strength & Conditioning and Cardio, these sessions are included in your membership but are also accessible on a drop-in basis. The aim is to have you train like an athlete, a world-class boxer and a champion. BXR brings authentic East End boxing to the majestic streets of Marylebone. The upstairs gym has a full size boxing ring as well as a plethora of equipment to work on functional, strength and cardio training. If combat training is your priority, they offer kickboxing, Muay Thai, MMA and Brazilian Jiu Jitsu, as well as circuits-based workouts. The changing rooms here are phenomenal, a real highlight. This really is the place to flex, punch, box n'roll - a knock-out venue!

POWER OF BOXING

THE ARCHES, 180 LAMBETH ROAD, LAMBETH, SE1 7JY

OPEN

SEE WEBSITE FOR TIMETABLE

 POWEROFBOXING.COM

 LAMBETH NORTH

Power of Boxing offers boxing-based fitness classes that last for a gruelling 60 minutes. Circuits-based and non-contact, you'll be doing a combination of cardio drills and technical pad work. Their high intensity workouts don't always feel good, but they certainly do good. Based in authentic venues across London, the trainers range from former amateur boxers to reformed offenders - so you can be sure that this is not the place to mess about. Their mission is to impact, empower and reform the lives of people that need the community and discipline of this sport. A noble cause to fight for.

THE RING BOXING CLUB

70 EWER STREET, SOUTHWARK, SE1 0NR

OPEN

MON-THU.	6:00AM - 9:00PM
FRI.	6:00AM - 8:00PM
SAT.	9:00AM - 3:00PM
SUN.	10:00AM - 1:00PM

 THERINGBOXINGCLUB.COM

 SOUTHWARK

Established in 1910, this boxing studio is situated in one of Southwark's railway arches, less than 100 yards from its notorious original site. Open to memberships as well as drop-ins, the 'Berserker' class is perfect for those that want to learn how to box but don't want to get hit. But HIIT (high intensity interval training) they do get! This class is taken by one of the pro team and features boxing circuits that work on stamina, speed and agility, putting those reflex reactions to the test. The gym features a large boxing ring in the centre as well as punch bags, indoor cycles, weights and sparring gloves. Suitable for beginners to advanced, The Ring is a great place release any pent-up energy and meet some fellow boxing friends. They also offer sparring classes for men and women - so get your white collar boxing gloves out.

ROONEY'S BOXING GYM

42 NEWINGTON CAUSEWAY, ELEPHANT AND CASTLE, SE1 6DR

OPEN

MON-FRI.   7:15AM - 9:00PM
SAT.   9:30AM - 4:00PM
SUN.   CLOSED

 ROONEYSGYMLONDON.COM

 ELEPHANT AND CASTLE

At Rooney's Boxing Gym you have to fight to get fit and get fit to fight. Though many of the classes are non-contact and purely fitness based, there are also white collar and women's sparring sessions for more advanced members keen to put their training to the test. Found on Newington Causeway, this is an immersive fitness experience that will teach you to float like a butterfly and sting like a bee. The open plan layout of the gym, with two large boxing rings in the centre and punchbags, indoor cycles and weights around the edge, make it an authentic and inspiring space to workout in. Incredibly good value, there is the option to 'pay-as-you-train' for a drop-in session, book a 1-2-1, or join as a member.

TOTAL BOXER

21 CRANFORD WAY, CROUCH END, N8 9DG

OPEN

MON-SUN.   7:00AM - 9:00PM

 TOTALBOXER.COM

 HORNSEY RAIL

While the benefits of boxing are huge, many are put off by the prospect of getting punched in the face. If this is you, then Total Boxer's signature one hour class 'Get Fit not Hit' is the perfect solution. Ideal for anyone looking to train like a fighter but avoid the fights, this class is focused on the exercises needed to improve and ensure fitness in the ring. With a custom-made boxing ring, a cardio area, a bag zone and a weights section, this converted warehouse space feels large and authentic. The second floor has an expansive studio used mainly for their BoxingYoga classes. The focus is on recovery and release, using moves and sequences that help stretch and strengthen muscles all over your body.

MARTIAL ARTS

DIESEL GYM
DIESEL GYM HQ, TOP FLOOR, SIMON HOUSE, BUTCHERS ROW, LIMEHOUSE, E1W 3HB

🌐 DIESELGYM.CO.UK

🚇 LIMEHOUSE

LONDON SHOOTFIGHTERS
620 WESTERN AVENUE, PARK ROYAL, W3 0TE

🌐 LONDONSHOOTFIGHTERS.COM

🚇 PARK ROYAL

NEW WAVE ACADEMY TRAINING CENTRE
38 HERMITAGE LANE, CROYDON, SE25 5HH

🌐 NEW-WAVE-ACADEMY.COM

🚆 SELHURST RAIL

FIGHT CITY GYM
15 WORSHIP STREET, OLD STREET, EC2A 2DT

🌐 FIGHTCITYGYM.CO.UK

🚇 OLD STREET / MOORGATE

THE MARTIAL ARTS PLACE
88 AVENUE ROAD, SWISS COTTAGE, NW3 3HA

🌐 THEMARTIALARTSPLACE.COM

🚇 SWISS COTTAGE

THE TOKEI CENTRE
28 MAGDALEN STREET, LONDON BRIDGE, SE1 2EN

🌐 TOKEICENTRE.ORG

🚇 LONDON BRIDGE

FIGHT ZONE
16 - 22 PRITCHARD'S ROAD, HACKNEY, E2 9AP

🌐 FIGHTZONELONDON.CO.UK

🚆 CAMBRIDGE HEATH RAIL

THE MMA CLINIC
29 - 30 ST ALBAN'S PLACE, ISLINGTON, N1 0NX

🌐 THEMMACLINIC.COM

🚇 ANGEL

URBAN WARRIORS ACADEMY
ARCH 12, MILES STREET, VAUXHALL, SW8 1RZ

🌐 URBANWARRIORSACADEMY.COM

🚇 VAUXHALL

LONDON FIGHT FACTORY
19 EBENEZER STREET, OLD STREET, N1 7LU

🌐 LONDONFIGHTFACTORY.COM

🚇 SHOREDITCH

MMA DEN
PAGDEN STREET, HAVELOCK TERRACE, ARCH 698, GLADSTONE COURT, BATTERSEA, SW8 4AT

🌐 MMADEN.COM

🚆 BATTERSEA PARK RAIL / QUEENSTOWN ROAD RAIL

XEN-DO MARTIAL ARTS
73 BAKER STREET, MARYLEBONE, W1U 6DJ

🌐 XEN-DO.COM

🚇 BAKER STREET

OUTDOOR SPACES

BASEFIT SHOREDITCH
BRAITHWAITE STREET,
SHOREDITCH, E1 6JU

OPEN
MON-FRI.   7:00AM - 8:00PM
SAT.   9:00AM - 11:00PM
SUN.   CLOSED

🌐 BASE-FIT.UK

🚇 SHOREDITCH HIGH STREET

BATTERSEA PARK
OUTDOOR GYM
BATTERSEA PARK, SW11 4NJ

🌐 WANDSWORTH.GOV.UK/
   BATTERSEAPARK

🚇 BATTERSEA PARK RAIL

BRITISH MILITARY FITNESS
MULTIPLE LOCATIONS
ACROSS LONDON

🌐 BRITMILFIT.COM

BROCKWELL LIDO
BROCKWELL PARK, DULWICH
ROAD, HERNE HILL, SE24 0PA

OPEN
VARIES THROUGHOUT SEASON

🌐 BROCKWELLLIDO.COM

🚆 NORTH DULWICH

KENNINGTON PARK
OUTDOOR GYM
KENNINGTON PARK ROAD,
KENNINGTON, SE11 4BE

OPEN
MON-SUN.   7:30AM - 9:30PM

🌐 KENNINGTONPARK.ORG

🚇 OVAL

PARLIAMENT HILL LIDO
PARLIAMENT HILL MANSIONS,
HAMPSTEAD HEATH, NW5 1NA

OPEN
MON-SUN.   7:00AM - 12:00PM

🌐 CITYOFLONDON.GOV.UK

🚇 GOSPEL OAK

PRIMROSE HILL
OUTDOOR GYM
PRIMROSE HILL, NW3 3AX

🌐 ROYALPARKS.ORG.UK

🚇 CHALK FARM /
   CAMDEN TOWN

SERPENTINE LIDO
HYDE PARK, SOUTH CARRIAGE
DRIVE, HYDE PARK, W2 2UH

OPEN
MON-SUN.   10:00AM - 6:00PM

🌐 SERPENTINELIDO.COM

🚇 KNIGHTSBRIDGE

SWIFT FITNESS
MULTIPLE LOCATIONS
ACROSS LONDON

🌐 SWIFTFITNESSGROUP.CO.UK

TOOTING BEC LIDO
TOOTING BEC ROAD, TOOTING,
SW16 1RU

OPEN
VARIES THROUGHOUT SEASON

🚆 STREATHAM

VICTORIA PARK
OUTDOOR GYM
VICTORIA PARK, GROVE ROAD,
SOUTH HACKNEY, E3 5TB

🌐 TOWERHAMLETS.GOV.UK

🚇 MILE END

WAKEUP DOCKLANDS
THE SHACK, WESTERN BEACH,
ROYAL VICTORIA DOCK,
SILVERTOWN, E16 1AG

OPEN
VARIES THROUGHOUT SEASON

🌐 WAKEUPDOCKLANDS.COM

🚇 WEST SILVERTOWN

ECOLE DE POLE

66 ROCHESTER PLACE, CAMDEN, NW1 9JX

OPEN

MON-FRI.	10:00AM - 10:00PM
SAT.	11:00AM - 4:00PM
SUN.	12:00AM - 2:30PM

 ECOLEDEPOLE.CO.UK

 CAMDEN TOWN

Down a rather inconspicuous lane between Camden and Kentish Town, Ecole de Pole is a cheeky little spot that's ready to show you some saucy moves and slinky manoeuvres. With sexy and classic pole choreo classes, as well as spinning pole, flexibility, pole flow and handstands, there's a range of choice to suit any student from beginner to advanced. The downstairs room has 8 poles (max. 2 per pole) which allows for an intimate setting and puts the newbies at ease. Whether you're looking to develop flexibility and strength, or just give something new and exciting a try, the pole classes here, as well as the aerial hoop and circus skills, are a good place start. Wear short shorts and a tank top to get a good grip on the pole. Impress your partner with your new moves!

FLIP OUT WANDSWORTH

BENDON VALLEY, EARLSFIELD, SW18 4LZ

OPEN

MON-SAT.	9:00AM - 10:00PM
SUN.	9:00AM - 9:00PM

 FLIPOUT.CO.UK

 EARLSFIELD

If you're looking for an unusual workout that's believed to be good for bone density, the lymphatic system and coordination, (as well as flippin' hilarious), then this is definitely the right place to bounce back into shape. Flipout Wandsworth, London's biggest trampoline park, is nothing short of genius. With 120 interconnected Olympic trampolines fitted into the floor, users have the freedom to jump, flip and twist here, there and everywhere around the room. Led by a well-trained instructor, the fitness classes are called 'Flip Fit Blast' (for 18 years and over) and work on flexibility and balance through a

combination of exercises taken from trampolining, parkour and gymnastics. Stay focussed in class or you'll find yourself in all sorts of compromising positions.

FLYING FANTASTIC

ARCH 27, OLD UNION YARD ARCHES, 229 UNION STREET, SOUTHWARK, SE1 OLR

OPEN

M, T + THU.	10:00AM - 9:00PM
WED + FRI.	7:45AM - 9:00PM
SAT.	9:45AM - 2:00PM
SUN.	11.50AM - 4:00PM

 FLYINGFANTASTIC.CO.UK

 SOUTHWARK

With four locations across London: Bankside, Battersea, Wimbledon and Old Street, the flagship of Flying Fantastic can be found in Arch 27 at the Old Union Yard Arches. A session here, whether it's in aerial skills, aerial hoop, static trapeze, aerial slings, aerial straps, conditioning and flexibility or aerial yoga will have you well on your way to joining Cirque du Soleil! With two fully equipped studios boasting wonderfully high ceilings, the atmospheric lighting makes for some seriously striking Insta uploads. Learning an impressive new skill is the main aim here, and your increase in strength, flexibility and overall fitness, comes as an inevitable by-product of practice and playing around. You'll be amazed at how you, and the time, fly. With drop-in classes every day and workshops held on a regular basis, the kind and welcoming community feel makes it easy to fit right in. If you're looking for an eccentric new hobby to tell your friends about, or to further refine your circus skills, Flying Fantastic is the height of cool!

HULAFIT

HUGH CUBITT CENTRE, COLLIER STREET, KING'S CROSS, N1 9QZ

OPEN

SEE WEBSITE FOR TIMETABLE

 HULAFIT.COM

 KING'S CROSS

HulaFit's form of exercise is low-impact and oh-so entertaining. The sessions last from 45 minutes to 1 hour and will have you spinning and shaking around the room. Using weighted hoops, you'll work your core muscles to keep it spinning around your waist. Your hoop is used as a prop to facilitate a full-body cardio workout. There's no doubt hula hooping helps strength, coordination and balance, but it also helps you let your hair loose and unwind at the end of a long day. Depending on the day of

the week, the classes take place in King's Cross, London Fields, Hackney, Westbourne Grove and Kennington. We suggest you wear trainers and fitness-friendly attire that lets you wiggle and giggle to the rhythm of the music.

HYDROFIT

137 NORTHCOTE ROAD, BATTERSEA, SW11 6PX

OPEN

SEE WEBSITE FOR TIMETABLE

 HYDROFIT.CO.UK

 CLAPHAM JUNCTION

Anyone trying HydroFit for the first time might find the bubbly experience slightly surreal, but there's no denying it does wonders for the derrière. The Battersea location is found on the Northcote Road towards the Wandsworth common, and contains individual hydro-bike pods that literally have you treading water. Sat on your aqua bike, the pod then fills up like a bath, rising just upward of the belly button. With a TV in front of you and wireless headphones to put on, you can choose to follow a more rigorous workout video, or leisurely watch any channel of your choice. In true jacuzzi style, 20 hydrojets massage your lower limbs while you peddle

away. This water-based form of exercise is particularly good for anyone that suffers from knee problems as no pressure is exerted on the joints.

MY AERIAL HOME

A2, BELL GREEN RETAIL PARK, BELL GREEN, SE26 4PR

OPEN

MON-THU.   11:00AM - 9:00PM
FRI.   11:00AM - 5:00PM
SAT.   10:00AM - 2:00PM
SUN.   10:00AM - 1:00PM
            (CHILDREN'S CLASSES)

 MYAERIALHOME.CO.UK

 LOWER SYDENHAM RAIL /
BELLINGHAM RAIL

Situated in a spacious warehouse within Bell Green Retail Park, this unique fitness gem is a little out of the way, but well worth the trek. My Aerial Home teaches a variety of aerial dance skills, including trapeze, rope, silks and hoop, plus ground-based skills that build balance and flexibility. The vibe is instantly welcoming, just as the name suggests. Guests walk straight into 'Mah's Kitchen' - a cosy café space decked out like a well-loved living room with soft furnishings and faux-fireplace. Most of the action happens in

the rigged studio, a cavernous space complete with plenty of colourful safety mats. There's a real communal feel, and with stories of students pursuing dance work around the world, it's clear that members are thoroughly supported.

VAUXWALL CLIMBING CENTRE

46 - 47A SOUTH LAMBETH ROAD, VAUXHALL, SW8 1SR

OPEN

MON-FRI.   6:00AM - 11:00PM
SAT-SUN.   9:00AM - 9:00PM

 VAUXWALLCLIMBING.CO.UK

 VAUXHALL

Did you know it's possible to improve the strength in your fingertips? Pulling yourself from one boulder to another improves this, along with muscular strength, power and co-ordination. At Vauxwall Climbing Centre you're encouraged to bring your friends and put your technique to the test. Set in four of the Vauxhall Arches, this indoor rock climbing space strips back the complicated ropes and harnesses, making it accessible for anyone to give a go. Sequences to boulder are set out in colour ranging from easy to extremely hard, but nothing is dangerous given the big padded mats below! No experience or expensive kit is needed, just

climbing shoes (available to hire in reception) and comfy clothes to let you bend and stretch in all directions. For many of the climbers, whether they know it or not, this is also an exercise in meditation. Total focus and unwavering concentration is needed to accomplish the task at hand and all other distractions are left off the mat.

YOGASPHERE

THE SHARD, 32 LONDON BRIDGE STREET, SOUTHWARK, SE1 9SG

OPEN

SEE WEBSITE FOR TIMETABLE

 YOGASPHERE.EU

 LONDON BRIDGE

Finding zen on floor 24 of the Shard tower is a wonderful way to end the day. YOGASPHERE offer yoga classes with a phenomenal view looking out over the glistening lights of London. Their Saturday 8:30am class moves up to floor 69, so get in there quickly to reserve a spot and take your practice to the very top. Mats are provided, so all you really need is a head for heights! There are no shower facilities, but there are private restrooms to get changed. Open to all levels, the class moves through a calming sequence of strong vinyasa poses and on warmer summer days it occasionally takes place on the open air 'Sky Deck' level 72. Said to be Europe's highest yoga class, you're given plenty of time to take in the panoramic views over the city before and after the hour of guided yoga flow. There's no better incentive to get that handstand straight than the iconic London skyline in the background, it makes for a breathtaking photo - one to impress your friends with over a fruity mocktail later on!

TOUGH MUDDER

INTERVIEW WITH WILL DEAN, CO-FOUNDER OF TOUGH MUDDER BY EILIDH HARGREAVES

Why have military-style workouts become popular over the last few years?

Tough Mudder is an event rather than a workout. You don't do Tough Mudder to get in shape - you get in shape to do a Tough Mudder. Recently, there has been a trend towards functional fitness. 10-15 years ago, most people thought a workout meant running or lifting weights and nothing else. Then CrossFit and HIIT workouts came along, and people started to understand that functional fitness is about being prepared for anything in life, rather than just being able to run a marathon. There has been a lot written about the benefits of exercise beyond the physical aspects, like extending life expectancy, boosting happiness levels, increasing productivity at work, and enhancing creativity. With society as a whole getting wealthier, people have developed a more nuanced understanding of fitness.

We live in a strange time. Everything that historically made up civic society is in decline: trade unions, political parties, church memberships, rugby clubs. And what's up? Gym membership. People aren't going for military-style workouts because they want to fight wars; they are doing it because in the military, there is a sense of collective purpose, teamwork and camaraderie. If you go to Soul Cycle in the US, it's almost like a church substitute. It's a workout, but there are also psychological and spiritual benefits of being part of it.

People are also looking for things they can do together with their friends. Whereas exercise is historically individual (if you do a marathon, people ask you what time you did, not who you did it with), Tough Mudder is all about getting through it as a team. Particular shared experiences are the new luxury good. Our parents' generation might have bragged about what car they had (or other material symbols of social status), but when you buy a car, its value depreciates. In contrast, particular experiences with your friends appreciate in value.

If someone is looking for an alternative 'gym' workout, why would this style be a good alternative?

For many, traditional gyms don't work anymore; they are boring, lonely and it requires a high degree of understanding of wellness and nutrition to get the most out of them. High-end group based workouts in London, like Barry's Bootcamp, are doing well because there are a lot of rich people (more than any other city in the UK) who can afford to spend £20 on a workout. Group-based workouts (with a good instructor and a varied exercise programme that gives you strength, conditioning, and cardio) are more likely to work because the workout is better, more social, and easy to fit into your schedule.

What are the differences between regular gym workouts and event-style obstacle courses?

We aren't claiming to to be a fitness business. We are saying that if you do a Tough Mudder, it'll be a great thing to help you achieve your goal. It's proven if you want to achieve a weight loss or muscular goal, having something in mind that you're going to try and do makes you more likely to achieve it, especially if it's with your friends. Obstacle style workouts happen in groups, sometimes outdoors, and don't generally involve a lot of stuff. I don't think it's a substitute to studio-based workouts, I think it's a compliment. If I go away on business, I'll still work out in the hotel gym - what's my alternative? But having something on top of that which you can do as part of a group is important.

What is the best training you can do to prepare yourself for military-style obstacle courses and endurance races?

If you can run five miles on your own relatively comfortably, you will be able to get around a Tough Mudder. It may not always be pretty, but you'll be able to get around. To train, you need to go running and you need to do upper body work. But you also need to come mentally prepared, with an attitude. There will be moments that will suck and moments that are fun, but at the end, you'll feel really proud of yourself. The biggest myth about Tough Mudder is that everyone who does it is an athlete. 2.5 million people have done it - almost 1 million in the UK alone. There aren't one million elite athletes in Britain, I am afraid. Tough Mudder is all about the team and getting through it.

What are the biggest changes in people's determination and participation you've seen?

Even 10 years ago, health, wellness and fitness was largely seen as something for men in their 20s and 30s. Compared to 5 years ago, a lot more women are doing events now, as well as people over the age of 40 and minorities. Fitness was seen as a rich (and in this country, white) person's thing. That has changed, which is great. People are also learning that you have to spend a long time on an elliptical machine to work off a cheeseburger, and that nutrition is at least 50%, if not 80%, of the battle.

Where do you see the future of the fitness events industry going?

People love mass participation events because they can do it with their friends. A little like marathons or Ironman, people come and do Tough Mudder because it's the biggest and the best; and it is so, because the most people do it. Now, the industry is changing, consolidating and professionalising, and safety standards are going up. The most dangerous part of doing a Tough Mudder is the drive to get there. You are seven times more likely to injure yourself in your car on the way. The event is very safe. With group based functional fitness, the results are superior. For that reason, it's here to stay.

FITNESS ON A SNEAKER STRING

BY **ZANNA VAN DIJK**

I'm Zanna, personal trainer, fitness blogger, Adidas ambassador, author of the book Strong and co-founder of the #girlgains movement. I am passionate about empowering women to love themselves and their bodies, and to get fit and healthy in a sustainable and enjoyable way. I am also a London-dweller and have been for the past two years. As a result, here are tonnes of recommendations for you on how to get fit in this buzzing city on a budget. Sure, London is full of luxurious boutique gyms, but what if you don't want to fork out £25 for a Pilates class and £7 for a green juice, I've got you covered.

3 OUTDOOR LONDON LOCATIONS TO GET FIT

Battersea Park

This is my favourite spot for an outdoor workout. One lap of the park is a 5km run, a perfect distance. Plus, you can stop off along the way at the outdoor gym to use the equipment and pull up bars. Battersea Park also has a beautiful pagoda with 3 sets of stairs on it, perfect for sprints and HIIT intervals.

Shoreditch

If you're bored of your usual running route, make a diversion through Shoreditch. The streets are full of incredible graffiti, which will provide some much-needed artistic distraction from your burning quads!

Primrose Hill

Primrose Hill is the ideal location for some sunrise hill sprints. Not only is it super steep and gets you sweaty in seconds, but you are rewarded for your hard work with an incredible panoramic view of the city. Instagram gold.

THE PARK BENCH WORKOUT

This circuit only requires you, a park bench and a positive attitude. Hop to it!

Complete each exercise for 30 seconds with 10 seconds' rest in-between. Repeat the circuit 3-5 times depending on how sweaty you want to get! Make sure you warm up and cool down sufficiently too.

+ **Box jumps**
+ **Incline Push Ups**
+ **Step Ups**
+ **Incline Mountain Climbers**
+ **Tricep Dips**

HOW TO STAY MOTIVATED WITHOUT AN EXPENSIVE GYM MEMBERSHIP

Plan Ahead
Schedule in your workouts and don't cancel on yourself. It's often best to do them first thing in the morning before your workload starts to creep up on you, as then you have fewer excuses to drop out!

Set Goals
It is much easier to stay motivated when you have a set goal to work towards. Whether that's an upcoming race, a physical challenge or a holiday abroad. Every time you want to quit, think about why you started.

Find Something You Enjoy
The easiest way to stay motivated to workout is to find a form of exercise you enjoy. Find your favourite. Whether that's doing Pilates videos in your bedroom or sprinting up the nearest hill. Whatever gives you that post workout buzz.

HOW TO MAKE FITNESS SOCIAL

Join A Local Park Run
These are free weekly runs around London parks. Not only do these build up a community, they provide you with motivation to push yourself when you're training, as you'll be running alongside others.

Start Your Own Group
Get your friends together and schedule in a weekly workout. You can do this outdoors or in your living room, just make sure you pop it in your diary like a doctor's appointment and don't cancel it.

Sign Up for A Challenge
Whether that's a race or an obstacle course, and do it with a buddy. That way you have a mutual goal you can work towards together. You can even make a joint training plan and keep each other on track.

HOW TO BE MORE ACTIVE EVERY DAY

Use Your Commute
You've heard this before, but your commute is the perfect opportunity to get moving. Hop off the tube or bus a stop early and walk the rest of the route home. If you're super keen you can even run to work or invest in a bike and cycle there. It works out cheaper in the long run.

Take Active Breaks
Your brain function will thank you. Take at least one break every hour, get up from your desk and go for a walk around the office; or outside if you can. This will refresh your mind as well as your body.

Get A Standing Desk
Or a swiss ball to sit on. This encourages you to challenge your core and engage more muscles, rather than slouching at a seated desk. Less back pain and better posture are the result. Most workplaces are eager to install this sort of equipment so don't be afraid to ask for it.

Use Your Lunch Break
And use it wisely. Get outdoors. Whether that's walking to a café that is a little further away, or getting on your kit and going for a 30 minute jog. Use this time to get your body moving and your blood flowing before you settle back down at your desk.

RUN CLUBS

ADIDAS 26RS
3 NORTON FOLGATE,
BISHOPSGATE, E1 6DB

🌐 RUNHUB.SWEATSHOP.CO.UK/
ADIDAS-26RS

ASICS RUNNING CLUB
CANARY WHARF, SOHO,
WEMBLEY

🌐 ASICS.COM/GB/EN-GB/
STORE-LOCATOR

GOOD GYM
PAVILION CAFÉ, VICTORIA
PARK, OLD FORD RD, E9 7DE

🌐 GOODGYM.ORG/MISSION-
RUNS

LDN BRUNCH CLUB
ROUTES ACROSS LONDON

🌐 LDNBRUNCHCLUB.CO.UK

MIDNIGHT RUNNERS
ROUTES ACROSS LONDON

🌐 MIDNIGHTRUNNERS.CO

NEVER STOP LONDON
NORTH FACE STORE, 290
REGENT STREET, W1B 3AP

🌐 FACEBOOK.COM/PG/
NEVERSTOPLONDON

NIKE+ RUN CLUB
ROUTES ACROSS LONDON

🌐 NIKE.COM/GB/EN_GB/C/
RUNNING/NIKE-RUN-CLUB

PROJECT AWESOME
CITY HALL, LONDON BRIDGE,
PRIMROSE HILL

🌐 PROJECTAWESOMEHQ.COM

RUN DEM CREW
ROUTES ACROSS LONDON

🌐 RUNDEMCREW.COM

RUNNER'S NEED
ROUTES ACROSS LONDON

🌐 RUNNERSNEED.COM

**SWEATSHOP RUNNING
COMMUNITY**
CITY, NOTTING HILL,
TEDDINGTON

🌐 RUNHUB.SWEATSHOP.CO.UK/
COMMUNITY/SWEATSHOP-
RUNNING-COMMUNITY

SWEATY BETTY
ROUTES ACROSS LONDON

🌐 SWEATYBETTY.COM

TRACK MAFIA
PADDINGTON RECREATION
GROUND, PADDINGTON,
W9 1PD

🌐 TRACKMAFIA.CO.UK

TRIBE COMMUNITY
ROUTES ACROSS LONDON

🌐 THIRDSPACE.LONDON/2016/02
/TRIBE-RUN-CLUB

ACTIVE IN STYLE

122 KING'S ROAD, CHELSEA, SW3 4TR

OPEN

MON-SAT.   10:00AM - 6:00PM

SUN.   12:00PM - 5:00PM

🌐 ACTIVEINSTYLE.COM

⊖ SLOANE SQUARE

Should you be looking for the latest in athleisure, Active in Style has got you sorted. Found right next to the boutique boxing studio KOBOX on the ever-so-stylish King's Road, this store has all you need for every possible exercise occasion. Whether you're kitting yourself out for a class at Paola's Bodybarre, indoor cycling at PSYCLE, or just a leisurely stroll through Chelsea - you've come to the right place. With looks imported all the way from Australia, LA and the east end of London, Active in Style curates looks from designers like Varley, P.E Nation, Lilybody and Onzie to offer a variety of activewear and its accessories. Whether you're working out in the studio or on the streets, on the common or the cross-trainer, it's likely that there's a piece of gear here to help you out. Their ethos involves creating a movement of fit, fearless women who are able to challenge and conquer their own limits, in serious style.

OPEN

MON–FRI.	10.30AM - 6.30PM
SAT.	10:00AM - 6:00PM
SUN.	12:00PM - 5:00PM

🌐 CAPEZIO.COM

⊖ COVENT GARDEN

CAPEZIO

ROYAL OPERA HOUSE, 33 ENDELL STREET, COVENT GARDEN, WC2H 9BA

For all things dance and performance related, Capezio is the place to find high-quality apparel and accessories for women, men and children. Whether for professional performance or just for fun, venture inside to discover a huge range of leotards, skirts, tights, shoes and activewear collections suitable for every dance and performance style. Capezio is renowned for exemplary products and a commitment to innovation, and has been for over 100 years - so you know you're in safe hands. The chic, modern exterior continues inside with thoughtfully designed layouts that make it easy to find exactly what you're looking for. And being conveniently located within London's vibrant performance district, Capezio couldn't be better situated for all West End studios and famous performance venues.

LIVE!

109A KING'S ROAD, CHELSEA, SW3 4PA

OPEN

MON-SAT.	10:00AM - 7:00PM
SUN.	12:00PM - 7:00PM

 LIVECLOTHING.UK

 SLOANE SQUARE

Bringing Brazil to the streets of Chelsea, LIVE! is one of the latest athleisure brands to set up shop on the King's Road. This lifestyle look has a particularly distinctive style, one that's growing in popularity and flair. You can't miss the explosive patterns and styles that are sold in this store. With items to match a variety of activities, LIVE! is designed to make you stand out in the crowds. Though the shop is small, the relaxed and personable atmosphere inside make it easy to try on

your favourite looks and swap sizes should you need. The contemporary style of the clothing inspires its wearers to move with the trends, LIVE! life in the present, Brazilian style!

LORNA JANE

6 SLINGSBY PLACE, ST MARTIN'S COURTYARD, COVENT GARDEN, WC2E 9AB

OPEN

MON-WED.	10:00AM - 7:00PM
THU.	10.00AM - 8.00PM
FRI-SAT.	10:00AM - 7:00PM
SUN.	12:00PM - 6:00PM

LORNAJANE.CO.UK

COVENT GARDEN

Lorna Jane's flagship UK store on Slingsby Place is a haven of fitness attire for every active woman. Looking to feel fantastic in high-tech, functional and oh-so-fashionable sportswear? Step inside for inspiring designs and long lasting, feel-good fabrics that will keep you motivated to train your way. Activewear is created specifically for women, using specially crafted fabrics, which are quick dry, breathable, shrink resistant and durable, and which come in a range of shapes and styles. Originating in Australia (sunny Sydney), Lorna Jane's desire to inspire women to lead fit and healthy

lifestyles - defined as 'active living' - goes beyond the shop floor and into the adjoining Active Living Room, where a range of strengthening and toning classes allow visitors to experience the philosophy first hand.

LULULEMON

187 - 191 REGENT STREET, SOHO, W1B 4JP

OPEN

MON-FRI.	10:00AM - 8:00PM
SAT.	10:00AM - 8:00PM
SUN.	12:00PM - 6:00PM

 LULULEMON.CO.UK

⊖ OXFORD CIRCUS

Lululemon's European flagship store can now be found in pride of place on bustling Regent Street. Based over two floors, this store offers high quality, technical fabrics that have been years in the making. As a yoga-inspired athletic apparel company originally from Vancouver, Lululemon sells activewear and accessories with names like 'Namastay Put' pants, 'Sunshine Salutation' bra and 'Roll with it' mats to celebrate the core focus of the brand. Sections for both women and men, Lululemon vend a lifestyle look that beautifully fuses comfort and style - great to workout in and easy to wear around town. On the upper level there is a Neat Nutrition shake bar, as well as a free photobooth to capture your excitement. There is also a large open area that gets cleverly converted into a studio for the complimentary in-store Yoga and HIIT classes, run on a weekly basis by the much admired Lululemon ambassadors. With customer service as slick as the store itself, the colour palette of neutral greys and marbles evokes a sense of calm and order - an urban retail retreat!

RAPHA LONDON

85 BREWER STREET, SOHO, W1F 9ZN

OPEN

MON-FRI.   8:00AM - 8:00PM

SAT.   8:30AM - 7:30PM

SUN.   11:00AM - 6:00PM

 RAPHA.CC

 OXFORD CIRCUS

The Rapha Clubhouse on Brewer Street is where Soho life meets cycle style, in a fashion store-cum-coffee shop. They play the latest cycle races on large screens in store so you're able to watch professionals manoeuvre around gruelling bends while you wait in line for your flat white. It is here that you'll find the sport and culture of road racing combine to entice a trendy bunch of bike fanatics. The buzz of this shop, along with technical design and comfortable feel of the Rapha

branded clothing, makes for an enjoyable shopping experience. Whether you're looking for cycle gifts, glasses or gear, or perhaps membership to their Rapha Cycling Club, you'll find it here.

SELFRIDGES

400 OXFORD STREET, MAYFAIR, W1A 1AB

OPEN

MON-FRI.   9:30AM - 9:00PM

SAT-SUN.   11:30AM - 6:00PM

SELFRIDGES.COM

BOND STREET

The Body Studio at Selfridges rarely gets it wrong. The impressive selection of sportswear brands range from Adidas to Ivy Park. Here they showcase the big names like Nike alongside some of the lesser-known up and coming boutique brands like P.E Nation and The Upside. Sports bras, skiwear, trainers and tops; walking round the third floor, they clearly take high-performance kit seriously. The transition from snazzy boxing gloves to stylish water bottles is seamless - just like

the ridiculously comfortable Lululemon leggings. Don't come here short of cash because the chances are you'll leave with a whole new wardrobe. There's no such thing as too many tank tops.

THE SPORTS EDIT

172 FULHAM ROAD, CHELSEA, SW10 9PR

Launched in 2015, The Sports Edit offers a stylish range of the latest activewear and sports accessories from around the world. As a multi-channel retailer, they sell a specially curated range of premium looks in-store and online, making it all too easy to mix and match leggings from LA with sneakers from New York. This flagship store is located on the fashionable Fulham Road, conveniently close to other healthy hotspots such as CPRESS and Lomax Chelsea. The outfits modelled here are those you're likely to spend your sporty Saturdays in - perfect for the post-run brunch date and afternoon outings with the pooch in hand. While it's not cheap to mix high performance with high-end fashion, The Sports Edit make it a necessity. As many couples meet in the gym, you should never look anything but your best.

SWEATY BETTY

40 - 40A LEDBURY ROAD, NOTTING HILL, W11 2AB

OPEN

MON-SAT.   10:00AM - 6:00PM

SUN.   12:00PM - 6:00PM

 SWEATYBETTY.COM

◒ NOTTING HILL GATE

How do you build a fierce community of stylish, active women, spanning from London to LA? Ask Tamara Hill Norton, British founder of now-cult sportswear and lifestyle brand Sweaty Betty. Inspired by the lack of choice of sportswear for women in the 90s - stores were filled with unflattering and badly suited masculine cuts - she and her husband Simon founded Sweaty Betty in 1998, opening a chic boutique in Notting Hill. Sweaty Betty aims to inspire women to find empowerment through fitness. Theirs are clothes for women who love fashion as much as fitness and adventure; those who want comfortable, high-tech gear, but still to keep ahead of trends. SB's products - from sports bras, to leggings and accessories - are styled as outfits. These looks, from Nomad, to Retreat and Boho (inspired by the free spirited traveller from the 1970s discovering the bohemian charms of Marrakech) encapsulate the holistic idea of lifestyle that SB seeks to enhance; workout gear is sold alongside casual clothes. Abundant in colourful, graphic prints, these multi-sport styles are super high tech; reversible looks offer savvy customers ingenious two-in-one buys. And if this isn't enough, Sweaty Betty stores also offer 70+ nationwide free in-store workout classes every week, which you can sign up to online. Which killer look will you bring?

HIGH STREET ACTIVEWEAR

ADIDAS
15 FOUBERT'S PLACE, SOHO, W1F 7QB

OPEN

MON-WED.	10:00AM - 7:30PM
THU-FRI.	10:00AM - 8:00PM
SAT.	10:00AM - 7:30PM
SUN.	12:00AM - 6:00PM

 ADIDAS.CO.UK

 OXFORD STREET

NEW BALANCE
287 - 291 OXFORD STREET, MAYFAIR, W1C 2DR

OPEN

MON-FRI.	9:30AM - 9:00PM
SAT-SUN.	12:00PM - 6:00PM

 NEWBALANCE.CO.UK

 OXFORD CIRCUS

NIKETOWN
236 OXFORD STREET, OXFORD CIRCUS, W1C 1DE

OPEN

MON-SAT.	10:00AM - 9:00PM
SUN.	11:30AM - 6:00PM

 NIKE.COM

OXFORD CIRCUS

PUMA
52 - 55 CARNABY STREET, SOHO, W1F 9QE

OPEN

MON-FRI.	10:00AM - 8:00PM
SAT.	10:00AM - 7:00PM
SUN.	12:00PM - 6:00PM

 PUMA.COM

 OXFORD CIRCUS / PICCADILLY CIRCUS

BALANCE FESTIVAL

INTERVIEW WITH LUDOVIC ROSSIGNOL-ISANOVIC, CREATOR AND CO-FOUNDER OF BALANCE FESTIVAL

What is Balance and what does it represent?

Balance Festival was born out of a dream to create the world's most exhilarating fitness and wellness festival. Aimed at busy urbanites seeking to achieve a healthier lifestyle, this event brings together well-travelled foodies, world-class fitness trainers, awe-inspiring yogis, and most of all, real people who share a common vision - to achieve a better self.

Our mission was to design an event that would be accessible, approachable and welcoming to all. We wanted to demystify the fads around wellness and deliver a highly inspirational, immersive and educational event, one that we would want to attend ourselves. Fundamentally, the festival has been designed to help Londoners step outside of their comfort zone and try something new.

What gap in the market did you see that you felt Balance Festival could fill?

London's fast-pace combined with a need to achieve our best self means we are seeing a major societal shift towards healthier lifestyle choices. But rather than reaching perfection, Londoners are on a quest to realise a fulfilling life balance.

On the one hand, you'll find the vast majority of Londoners confused by all the fads but eager to make a sustainable health-oriented change in their lifestyle - these are Balance Seekers who only need a little push to embark on their journey of wellness. On the other hand, you'll find the Urban Healthies - those that are well-informed, inquisitive and savvy, already well advanced in their wellness journey. For the non-initiated, signing up for a first HIIT or yoga class can be intimidating and it's that first small step that has the power to lead to long lasting life changes. With Balance, we are removing the daunting barriers to entry by offering a fully comprehensive experiential programme covering all aspects of food, fitness and wellness - to ultimately help Londoners embark onto their wellness journey.

What makes Balance so unique?

We are lucky enough to have a wonderful selection of industry experts, nutritionists and personal trainers on board, all of whom add something completely unique to the festival. The People of Balance represent a hand-picked selection of real, inspirational Londoners who've made a name for themselves within the food, fitness and wellness communities. Predominantly, we seek out contributors who genuinely share our vision to help people achieve a more fulfilling life balance and challenge the status quo.

Tell us about your life journey and how this inspired Balance.

My personal fitness and wellness revolution started four years ago, when I took on running seriously. Before this, I had injured myself and my fitness levels were at an all-time low. Competing in the London Marathon got me back on track. I then started training in various boutique fitness studios around London - I got totally addicted to the infectious energy of their workouts. It completely changed the way I used to train and has led me to explore new practices and ways of exercising.

Producing events has always been in my DNA - from running gigs in Belgium when I was younger to launching coffee festivals around the world with my business partner. I've always had a fundamental passion for bringing like-minded people together and producing highly engaging events. Creating something new from scratch is highly stimulating and creating the Balance concept has been incredibly rewarding. It unites my passions together: delicious food, good music, boundary-pushing fitness workouts, inspirational people, cutting-edge educational content and sharp design - all under one roof!

What is your daily fitness and nutrition regime?

I try to exercise three to four times a week and keep my regime varied. Researchers have found that people are more likely to adhere to HIIT sessions, as they are one of the most time effective and fun ways to get your fitness fix, burn calories and build muscle. I often run to work, aside from the health benefits, it's a form of meditation for me. I try to integrate mindful practices into my life, be it a daily 10-minute meditation before dinner or simply banning digital devices from the bedroom.

My advice for maintaining a healthy diet is to eat nutrient dense food that you actually enjoy. There is no point in eating healthily if you don't like the taste of the food on your plate. Healthy food doesn't have to be boring and bland. I do however enjoy a glass of red wine or two, which is absolutely fine, everything in moderation.

What are your predictions for the future of health and wellness?

I believe we'll see more and more bespoke nutrition and training programmes, more people adopting mindful practices within everyday life and the science behind sleep will be better understood. Bio-individuality plays a key role here of course - it's all about finding what works for you and your body, and most importantly, finding a way of life that is healthy, sustainable and enjoyable.

What's next for Balance?

Our vision is to launch Balance Festivals all around the world: New York, LA, Amsterdam, Sydney and Melbourne are in the pipeline and perhaps a ski resort or two along the way for a winter edition of Balance Festival.

MIND
BODY
SOUL

SPAS, MINDFUL SPACES + INSPIRATION

AGUA BATHHOUSE AND SPA AT THE MONDRIAN

MONDRIAN LONDON, 20 UPPER GROUND, BANKSIDE, SE1 9PD

OPEN

MON-SUN.   9:00AM - 8:00PM

 MORGANSHOTELGROUP.COM

SOUTHWARK

In keeping with the transatlantic shipping roots of the famed Sea Containers building, Agua Bathhouse and Spa at the Mondrian (lower ground floor) submerges you below water level and whisks you away to a white washed nirvana. Upon entrance, you'll notice the delight is in the details with textured walls and curved sofas representing the tranquil movement of waves. The design is minimalist and uncluttered, creating a spotless aesthetic to keep the mind free from distraction. The Glamour Lounge and relaxation room (with scooped loungers) encourage guests to put their worries to one side and enjoy a post-treatment snooze. With 5 treatment rooms and a Hammam, the signature Soveral experience facial is the recommended must. Agua Bathhouse and Spa embraces the theme of integrative health, with training and treatments on chronic pain and 'wellness for cancer'. And on a more uplifting note, their 'Spa Social' evening happens once a month and includes relaxing music, healthy food bowls, herbal tea and use of the facilities - it's one to book with your friends for a night out you'll actually remember!

OPEN

MON-FRI.   9:00AM - 9:00PM

SAT-SUN.   9:00AM - 8:00PM

 MORGANSHOTELGROUP.COM

 OXFORD CIRCUS

AGUA BATHHOUSE AND SPA AT THE SANDERSON

50 BERNERS STREET, FITZROVIA, W1T 3NG

The Agua Spa at the Sanderson must be looked at within the historical context of the building itself in order to be fully appreciated and admired. Previously the headquarters and showroom for Arthur Sanderson and Sons, manufacturers of wallpaper, fabrics and paint, the building is now Grade-II listed and the Agua Spa has been designed to incorporate this artistic history. Set up using miles of hanging diaphanous white curtains, there are 14 all-white treatment rooms, a chill-out zone with chairs, loungers and cosy meditation pods. Besides its rather surreal and floaty ambiance, there is a calming absence of noise which does wonders for the senses. There is a special grooming lounge for hands, feet, brows and tinting treatments as well as a well kitted out gym for a sweaty workout. The list of treatments involves massage, face and body, and in special collaboration with the Sanderson, the Eve Lom Signature Facial is carried out by renowned therapist Eve Lom herself!

AKASHA HOLISTIC WELLBEING CENTRE
AT HOTEL CAFÉ ROYAL 50 REGENT STREET, SOHO, W1B 5AS

OPEN

MON-FRI.	6:30AM - 10:00PM
SAT.	8:00AM - 10:00PM
SUN.	8:00AM - 10:00PM

 HOTELCAFEROYAL.COM

PICCADILLY CIRCUS

Once you've entered Akasha Holistic Wellbeing Centre, never in a million years would you guess that you're only minutes away from the touristy hub of Piccadilly Circus. For what Akasha lacks in size, it makes up for in quality and variety. Boasting a spa, gym, yoga studio and lounge space, Akasha also adds meditation and fitness classes to the mix. Promoting a more holistic approach to health and relaxation, their broad range of treatments, scrubs and massages are popular among city visitors, and workers in the West End. Down the cream marble stairs waits the vibrant turquoise 18m pool with loungers around the edge. Any treatment over 80 minutes gains you access to enjoy these facilities. With a range of specialist hydrotherapy treatments, including Watsu sessions, Vichy shower treatments, and private Hammam experiences, you're simply spoilt for choice. The Detoxifying Vichy Ritual is highly recommended too, using the pressure of six water jets to release tension whilst you're being massaged, it's hard to think of anywhere nicer to be!

AMAN SPA AT THE CONNAUGHT HOTEL

CARLOS PLACE, MAYFAIR, W1K 2AL

OPEN

MON-SUN.   9:00AM - 9:00PM

 THE-CONNAUGHT.CO.UK

 BOND STREET / GREEN PARK

Part of the Connaught Hotel in swanky Mayfair, a plush mirrored lift takes you down to the Asian-inspired Aman Spa. The tranquil vibe and simple decor sets the tone for a relaxing and enjoyable spa experience. The pool is 29 degree heated with chlorine-free water, using instead a natural ionic solution with a UV system to keep it clean. The relaxation loungers are perfectly positioned to face you toward the cascading granite water wall and subsequently soothe the senses. There is a unisex steam room infused with essential oils and lemongrass, with ginger tea on hand to ensure you feel fresh both inside and out. With a whole host of specialist complimentary therapies and stunning beauty services to choose from in any one of their five low-lit treatment rooms, there's plenty to keep you coming back for more.

BHUTI

50 HILL RISE, RICHMOND, TW10 6UB

OPEN

MON-FRI.   9:00AM - 9:00PM
SAT.   9:00AM - 7:00PM
SUN.   9:00AM - 6:00PM

 BHUTI.CO

 RICHMOND

Find sanctuary on Richmond Hill inside Bhuti; an oasis of wellness. Bhuti is a holistic wellness space, containing a 100% certified organic café, two yoga studios, consultation and treatment rooms, two members' lounges, a downstairs hand and foot massage room and a retail area (selling vegan makeup and yoga kit, amongst other treats). Bhuti's single aim is to make sure you leave their doors feeling like you - useful in busy London, where time so often gets the better of us. The two studios host yoga, Pilates and HIIT training, accommodating between 6 and 20 people per class. If you just want to catch a break, the member areas are the perfect relaxation spot, where you can lie down, sway in hanging nest chairs, or work from desks, providing an alternative home workspace. As the saying goes: 'Bhuti lies within'.

THE BULGARI SPA

171 KNIGHTSBRIDGE, KNIGHTSBRIDGE, SW7 1DW

OPEN

MON-FRI.   9:00AM - 10:00PM

SAT-SUN.   9:00AM - 9:00PM

 BULGARIHOTELS.COM

 KNIGHTSBRIDGE

Exclusive and oh-so-sleek, the Bulgari Hotel Spa takes glitz and glamour to a luxurious new level. Arranged over two floors, this spa is part of the Bulgari Hotel, located in the heart of affluent Knightsbridge. The wood-lined spa reception is noise and clutter free with an extensive range of products as the central focus of one well-lit wall. Boasting 11 private treatment rooms and 1 double spa suite, complete with its own steam room and Jacuzzi; the wellness therapies here are holistic in their approach and aim to treat the outside to rebalance and realign the inside. The 25m colonnaded swimming pool is surrounded by lounges, cabanas and a vitality pool, covered by gold leaf tiles. This spoiling scene makes it easy to feel as though you've quietly slipped off on a glorious Grecian luxury getaway!

COMO SHAMBHALA URBAN ESCAPE
AT THE METROPOLITAN HOTEL   19 OLD PARK LANE, MAYFAIR, W1K 1LB

OPEN

MON-SUN.   9:00AM - 9:00PM

 COMOHOTELS.COM

 HYDE PARK CORNER

The Como Shambhala Urban Escape Spa is a porthole to the relaxation space you've been searching for. The sleek, minimalist interior of this spa resonates with its Asian roots and contemporary style. If you've booked in for a treatment there's a crisp white robe waiting for you, as well as soft slippers and a neatly stacked pile of green apples in the spa reception. With Manuka honey, lemon and ginger tea offered upon arrival and again after your treatment, this warm herbal infusion sets a deliciously soothing tone. There are 6 treatment rooms, 2 of which are doubles with steam rooms, as well as a gym and an array of treatments to choose from. The

focus here is on holistic health and wellbeing, with a results driven approach that looks to tackle any underlying aches and pains. This is the place to come for anyone with an interest in alternative treatments, they hold workshops and retreats, as well as consultations with experts on intuitive healing, structural integration and mind and body balance.

COWSHED PRIMROSE HILL

115 - 117 REGENT'S PARK ROAD, PRIMROSE HILL, NW1 8XP

OPEN

MON-WED.	9:00AM - 8:00PM
THU-FRI.	9:00AM - 9:00PM
SAT.	9:00AM - 7:00PM
SUN.	9:30AM - 5:00PM

 COWSHEDONLINE.COM

 CHALK FARM

You'll find this café-salon fusion store packed out on weekends, and rightly so. Beautifully kitsch and well-placed in the heart of Primrose Hill, Cowshed is the perfect meeting place for a catch up with friends or a pamper session. As you come into the shop, peek around the corner to catch a glimpse of the upstairs spa area (an additional seven treatment rooms are located downstairs). Mini retro televisions play in front of gorgeous - and humongous - blue mani-pedi chairs - an idyllic way to relax in a beautifully designed spot. We recommend Evening Primrose Body Wrap, a 90-minute ultra-indulgent full body treatment, but if you're time-poor, best try the Speedy Facial for a quick replenish. The café compliments the spa nicely. It serves simple, nutritious food in a relaxed, communal environment. A mix of large sharing tables and smaller tables for two establishes an at-home, easy vibe. On your way out give in to temptation at the retail area; crammed full with Cowshed lotions and potions, it's hard to leave without a little extra treat.

THE DORCHESTER SPA

53 PARK LANE, MAYFAIR, W1K 1QA

OPEN

MON-SAT.   7:00AM - 9:00PM

SUN.   8:00AM - 9:00PM

 DORCHESTERCOLLECTION.COM

 HYDE PARK CORNER

The Dorchester Spa is certainly the place for anyone looking to indulge in some premium pampering. Inspired by the opulent 1930s Art Deco style of The Dorchester Hotel, the candy cream hues of the Spatisserie, which offers light lunches and luxury afternoon tea, is a lavish welcome to your spa experience. The Carol Joy hair salon and manicure and pedicure suite make this the perfect place for celebratory hen parties or perhaps a mother-daughter day out. The Spa has 9 treatment rooms, including 2 double suites, which are kept to a more minimalist style. They also have male and female aromatic steam rooms and a joint relaxation room, with daily newspapers to allow for some quiet time out. The Dorchester Spa Signature Facial by Carol Joy London lasts for 60 minutes and uses organic golden millet oil and a pure collagen mask to enrich and brighten the complexion. This is a great choice for anyone looking to rejuvenate dull skin. Open every day of the year except for Christmas, this indulgent option will have you feeling pampered like the princess you are.

ESPA LIFE AT CORINTHIA HOTEL

WHITEHALL PLACE, EMBANKMENT, SW1A 2BD

OPEN

MON-FRI.   6:30AM - 10:00PM

SAT-SUN.   7:30AM - 10:00PM

🌐 ESPALIFEATCORINTHIA.COM

⊖ EMBANKMENT

The first thing you'll notice when you enter the ESPA Life spa at Corinthia hotel is the aromatic scent that guides you to the reception desk. The cream marble surroundings along with the serene silver artwork and flickering fireplace, sets a tranquil tone - one that instantly wipes the central London commute from your mind. Set over four floors, ESPA Life at Corinthia offers a combination of spa treatments, complementary alternative therapies, fitness, nutrition, beauty and hair by Daniel Galvin. The thermal floor and wet area includes a dramatic amphitheatre sauna, a steam room, a Vitality Pool with water massage jets, marble heated lounges and splendid relaxation bays. And while the luxurious pool and opulent ice fountain are particularly photogenic features, there is a strict no phones policy on this floor to ensure discretion as well as a digital detox! ESPA Life offers an impressive array of treatments, from facials to physiotherapy, inclusive of men, as well as mums-to-be. Attracting the international traveller with stylish little sleep pods, ESPA Life is the perfect solution to that tiresome jetlag.

THE HOUSE OF ELEMIS

2 LANCASHIRE COURT, MAYFAIR, W1S 1EX

OPEN

MON-SAT.   10:30AM - 9:00PM
SUN.   10:00AM - 6:00PM

 ELEMIS.COM

 BOND STREET

When it feels like there's no time to relax, that's where The Speed Spa at The House of ELEMIS comes into its own. The perfect solution for busy professionals, this works on your eyes, face and neck in just 30 minutes (or 15 if you're really pushed for time). With a range of options to soothe, moisturise and massage the skin in a matter of moments, you'll leave feeling softer than a cashmere coat. Removed from the busy hustle and bustle of the packed pavements, this townhouse has 5 treatment rooms, and a luxurious penthouse suite. Especially known for its biotech treatments, The House of ELEMIS is quick to inform you that this is 'where spa meets science meets skin'.

SOHOLISTIC SPA AT THE HAM YARD HOTEL

ONE HAM YARD, SOHO, W1D 7DT

OPEN

MON-SUN.   9:00AM - 7:00PM

 FIRMDALEHOTELS.COM

 PICCADILLY CIRCUS

Ham Yard Hotel is one of London's oh-so-secret escapes, found just a few minutes' walk from Piccadilly Circus. Their Soholistic Spa on the lower ground floor offers a range of body and beauty treatments. With 2 single treatment rooms and 1 double, you can enjoy a massage alone or book a romantic spa day with your partner. Any long-lasting treatment allows you access to the relaxation room, steam room, gym or the specially designed hypoxic studio. If you've booked yourself in for one of their signature deep tissue sports massages, you can combine it with an intensive workout beforehand. The space itself has been tastefully designed by Kit Kemp and fuses together a combination of textures, patterns and cultural relics that truly reflects the holistic world of wellness. Refreshed and re-energized, Soho awaits for an early dinner.

THE SPA AT FOUR SEASONS PARK LANE

HAMILTON PLACE, MAYFAIR, W1J 7DR

OPEN

MON-SUN.   8:00AM - 10:00PM

 FOURSEASONS.COM

 HYDE PARK CORNER

On the top floor of the luxurious Four Seasons Hotel, the view from the spa is a relaxation treatment in itself. With floor to ceiling windows, the waiting area and nail salon look over Hyde Park, London's green oasis. The combination of natural light, calming aromatherapy scents and soothing music send you in to a peaceful gaze across the city. The facilities here are separated by gender, but both have state-of-the-art steam room, sauna and vitality pool to regulate body temperature (suitable for pregnant women). With a large number of relaxation pods and specially fitted showers to mimic a rainforest, it's not hard to see why this has been rated a 5* spa. The Sky Suite is the crème de la crème, a couples' treatment room that makes the most of the breath-taking views. With a private double steam shower, a separate dressing room and a relaxation area, it's the perfect present for your other half. Any 60-minute treatment also gives you access to the facilities, including the recently renovated gym and the café/lounge area. Rumour has it that the bespoke massages are just as good as the view!

SPA ILLUMINATA

63 SOUTH AUDLEY STREET, MAYFAIR, W1K 2QS

OPEN

MON.	10:00AM - 6:00PM
TUE.	10:00AM - 7:00PM
WED-THU.	10:00AM - 9:00PM
FRI-SAT.	10:00AM - 7:00PM
SUN.	10:00AM - 6:00PM

 SPAILLUMINATA.COM

 GREEN PARK

You don't walk into Spa Illuminata, you float. The bright entrance with its white and gold colour scheme sets the decadent tone for the rest of the spa. As majestic as Mayfair itself, the Roman style design continues downstairs with the cream marble walls and mosaic tiled floors. Dressed in your fluffy white robe and matching slippers, the Temple of Relaxation feels fit for an Empress. Come here for a day to yourself. With 2 steam rooms

and 8 treatment rooms, we recommend booking in for one of their packages. The Goddess Treatment is 5 hours of heavenly bliss.

THE SPA AT MANDARIN ORIENTAL

66 KNIGHTSBRIDGE, KNIGHTSBRIDGE, SW1X 7LA

OPEN

MON-FRI.	9:00AM - 10:00PM
SAT-SUN.	9:00AM - 9:00PM

 MANDARINORIENTAL.COM

 KNIGHTSBRIDGE

Where to begin with the Spa at the Mandarin? With 8 treatment rooms (all with private showers), male and female sanariums, vitality pools and amethyst crystal steam rooms, they hold nothing back in their offering of premium facilities for relaxation. Spread over two floors, the décor is sleek and contemporary, with dark interiors and a cool grey slate that surrounds the expansive blue swimming pool. A few laps here will leave you feeling refreshingly composed - the

peaceful ambiance allows you to float away in your own thoughts. This is the perfect physical and mental escape for anyone looking to zone out of the everyday.

THE SPA AT ST. PANCRAS RENAISSANCE LONDON HOTEL
EUSTON ROAD, KING'S CROSS, NW1 2AR

OPEN

MON-SUN.   9:00AM - 9:00PM

 STPANCRASLONDON.COM

 KING'S CROSS ST. PANCRAS

Situated on the lower ground floor of the stunning St Pancras Renaissance Hotel, this spa is a relaxation station. Packages cater for people partaking in long tiresome journeys with names like 'Time Traveller', 'Voyage Recovery', 'Ticket to Tranquillity', 'Arrive and Revive' and 'High Time for Tea Time' to help you relax and unwind. The Victorian-inspired spa has 6 treatment rooms, this includes one for couples and a 'beauty room' for hands and feet. The colour scheme is mainly marbles and muted browns though the relaxation pool is particularly decorative. The spa also has a steam room, Jacuzzi, hot sauna and loungers around the side for you to lie back and absorb the calming ambiance.

URBAN RETREAT AT HARRODS
5TH FLOOR, HARRODS, 87 - 135 BROMPTON ROAD, KNIGHTSBRIDGE, SW1X 7XL

OPEN

MON-SAT.   10:00AM - 9:00PM

SUN.   11.30AM - 6:00PM

 URBANRETREAT.CO.UK

 KNIGHTSBRIDGE

In line with the glitz and glamour of Harrods, this luxurious Urban Retreat Spa on the fifth floor does not disappoint. With 41 styling stations, 21 beauty rooms, 16 manicure and pedicure stations, a make-up salon and a picture perfect Moroccan Hammam, as well as an Urban Retreat organic Café, there's no shortage of ways in which to have oneself well and truly pampered. You'll notice that the treatment list is so large that it's actually a book, so it's useful to glean recommendations from the knowledgeable staff on the front desk. Given that this is probably the biggest luxury salon in Europe, there really is everything you could possibly need all in one place - be that a slimming body treatment, lash extensions, hair analysis by Ricardo Vila Nova, or perhaps even a soft-lift facial? The Moroccan Hammam is a slice of paradise... see for yourself!

COMPLEMENTARY THERAPIES

BY **THE LONDON WELLNESS GUIDE**

Complementary therapies are able to work alongside conventional medicine to assist the healing process, help manage symptoms and enhance a greater sense of wellbeing. For anyone looking for a natural way to feel more balanced in body and mind, complimentary therapies can be hugely beneficial. Some are rooted in thousands of years of practice and tradition and are regulated and accessible via the NHS, although many have little scientific backing and have not been proven to cure illness or disease. Therapies are usually risk-free, and offer effective ways to relieve pain, stress and other emotional and physical disorders, while also relaxing and uplifting both body and mind. The most important thing is to find what works best for you.

BODYWORK THERAPIES

Acupuncture

Acupuncture originates from East Asia and has been central to traditional Chinese Medicine for 2,000 years. Many qualified health practitioners now practise a modern interpretation, known as Western Medical Acupuncture, which is available on the NHS. Treatment involves inserting very fine, sterile needles into specific parts of the body in order to stimulate the body's natural healing response. Traditionally, this is thought to help balance the body's vital energy, known as Qi, and free 'energy blockages', believed to lead to sickness and disease. In Western medicine, acupuncture is shown to stimulate nerves to release chemical substances that reduce physical symptoms, relieve pain and enhance wellbeing. Many people find that acupuncture leaves them feeling happier and more relaxed after treatment.

Chiropractic

Chiropractic is a manual practise similar to Osteopathy. The emphasis is on spinal and joint manipulations with the aim of restoring the bones, muscles and joints to their natural places. Sessions may include X-rays and MRI scans of the spine and affected joints, physical stretches, massage and hot and cold treatment. Occasionally acupuncture, electrical current or laser treatment is used to stimulate the body's natural healing process. Chiropractors are likely to prescribe exercises and self-care, which patients can do at home. Chiropractic care is thought to help relieve pain, headaches, tension, back pain, and head and neck problems. It is a regulated healthcare profession and can be accessed through many GP surgeries.

Osteopathy

Osteopathy is based on the principle that the body is healthier and will heal more effectively when the musculoskeletal system is in alignment. An Osteopath will manipulate the bones and muscles to improve the way the body moves, which will reduce pain. Using their hands, a therapist will move, stretch and massage particular parts of the body, sometimes rhythmically working on joints or making short, sharp manipulations called 'velocity thrusts' to ensure correct alignment. Osteopathic treatment can improve circulation, reduce swelling, ease pain and restore movement, and is generally considered beneficial to health and wellbeing - GP surgeries are increasingly offering access to osteopathy.

Reflexology

Originally developed by the Ancient Egyptians, Reflexology has been used for centuries to help relieve a variety of problems, including stress, pain, insomnia and digestive issues. The practice is based on the idea that the body can be mapped through the feet, with the left foot corresponding to the left side of the body and the right foot corresponding to the right. Practitioners aim to treat the body as a whole by applying pressure to specific areas of the feet, hands and sometimes ears, in order to target particular organs and trigger the body's natural healing responses. Their focus is on healing both the symptoms and their causes. There is no scientific evidence that Reflexology can help treat medical conditions, but it can be an effective way to help manage pain, cope with stress and anxiety, and achieve a greater sense of wellbeing.

Reiki

Reiki (meaning 'universal energy' in Japanese) is a form of 'acupressure' originating from Japan in the 20th century. The aim is to change and balance energy fields, or 'Qi', in and around the body to help relieve physical, psychological and emotional discomfort. Similar to acupuncture, this practise is thought to rid the body of 'energy blockages' and stimulate the natural healing process. Reiki therapists will place their hands either on, or just above, the body - usually starting with the top of the head and working their way down to the feet. They may stop to focus on particular areas, and it is possible to feel a warmth, coolness or tingling sensation while the therapist works. Reiki healing is particularly helpful for relaxation and to improve emotional wellbeing, but there is no established evidence that it can cure or prevent disease.

Shiatsu

Shiatsu is an ancient Japanese massage art and form of 'acupressure'. Similar to Reiki, it works with the principle that the body's energy flows through channels called meridians, and that any disruption to that energy flow can lead to illness and disease. Practitioners will use their hands, arms, legs and even feet to apply pressure to particular points on the meridian channels with the aim of increasing blood flow, releasing toxins and tension, and stimulating the hormonal system. By doing so, the body is encouraged to heal itself and restore balance. There is no evidence to suggest that Shiatsu can help cure or prevent disease, but many people turn to this form of massage therapy to alleviate stress and tension, relieve pain and enhance happiness and wellbeing.

ALTERNATIVE MEDICINAL THERAPIES

Aromatherapy

Aromatherapy is the use of essential oils to boost wellbeing, relieve stress and revitalise the body. There are over 400 essential oils in total, taken from the flowers, fruits, seeds, leaves, roots and bark of certain plants. Essential oils can be diluted and massaged into the body, diffused with an oil burner, or dabbed onto a handkerchief or pillowcase. Some oils are also believed to have additional healing properties, including treating pain, infection, inflammation and burns.

There are two ways in which oils are believed to help people feel better - first is their ability to be absorbed into the skin, which may help soothe or heal tissues. Second is the effect of aromas on the brain, which can spark both physical and emotional responses; lavender as an aid for sleep is a common example. There may not be any concrete evidence that aromatherapy can treat illness, but essential oils offer an effective, natural way to reduce symptoms such as stress and anxiety, and enhance overall wellbeing.

Ayurveda

Ayurvedic Medicine is an ancient system of care originating from India and practised for around 5,000 years. The word 'Ayerveda' literally translates as 'life knowledge' and is based on the idea that mind and body are inextricably linked. Practitioners will use a range of techniques to manage ill health, including dietary recommendations, massage, herbal medicine, meditation, yoga and breathing exercises. The overall aim is to expand self-awareness, restore balance in the mind and extend this sense of balance to the body in order to heal. Practitioners advocate restful sleep, a colourful diet and living in tune with nature. Although Ayurvedic Medicine isn't scientifically proven, certain aspects - such as meditation and yoga - have been shown to reduce stress levels and enhance wellbeing.

Chinese Herbal Medicine

Chinese Herbal Medicine is part of a system of medicine commonly known as Traditional Chinese Medicine (TCM). TCM, which also includes acupuncture, massage, breath work and Tai Chi, is thought to date back to the 3rd Century BC and is still used alongside conventional medicine in Chinese state hospitals today. Through prescribing various plant, mineral and occasionally animal-based remedies, the practitioner aims to restore the body's vital energy flow (Qi) and improve physical and mental health. Plants will be chosen according to their taste, how they affect the body, or how they interact with the body's energy. Commonly used plants include Echinacea (for immunity), St John's Wort (for depression) and ginger (for nausea). Practitioners will take the whole body into account, examining everything from heart rate to skin condition, before prescribing fresh herbs (for tea), tinctures, tablets or ointments.

Homeopathy

Homeopathy is based on the theory that you can treat 'like with like'. Remedies contain miniscule quantities of substances that in larger doses would in fact cause the symptoms that they aim to treat. Practitioners believe that taking substances in their heavily diluted form triggers the body's natural healing reaction and help alleviate symptoms. Homeopathy is commonly seen as a natural, drug-free way to cope with stress, anxiety, depression, pain, sickness, fatigue and various other complaints, but it is not known whether this is down to the effectiveness of remedies or the power of the placebo effect. There are several homeopathic hospitals in the UK and some medical doctors are trained in homeopathy, but there is no concrete evidence to suggest that homeopathy can be used on its own to treat illness or disease.

MASSAGE: THE SURPRISING BENEFITS OF THIS ANCIENT TECHNIQUE BY THE LONDON WELLNESS CENTRE

We all do our best to be fit and healthy these days - whether that's upping our water intake, cutting down on sugar or hoping that our excessive Instagram swiping will find us the new 'holy grail' of wellness. The reality, however, is that our daily schedule has more of an impact on our bodies than we realise. Long hours spent hunched over a computer at our desks means we rarely get the flexibility our bodies crave (ideally we should be standing and stretching every 20-30 minutes!). Compensating this with a long, intense session in the gym afterwards is actually counterproductive. This results in a tight, injury-prone body.

Massage is an excellent way to help counteract the physical - and mental - stresses and strains we put ourselves under. Being 'selfish' once had negative connotations - but this term is being reclaimed by more and more people who understand its benefits. The old-age adage of 'you can't look after anyone else before you look after yourself' is evident for any of us who have burned the midnight oil. Everyone knows of someone who has fallen ill after an intense period at work. We've all been there; we've vowed to reassess our work/life balance, and yet time and time again people are sucked back into the vortex of a hectic work schedule, barely etching out time to exercise, cook or even unwind.

Self-care - of which massage is a great example - should be a non-negotiable in our lives, like brushing our teeth or eating breakfast. With the rise of the health and wellness industry in the last decade or so, massage is becoming a vital supplement to people's fitness and wellbeing, no matter what age.

Studies have found that massage can have a profound impact on a variety of physical and mental conditions; from headaches, RSI, chronic fatigue through to IBS, arthritis and depression. Through careful manipulation of soft tissues of the body, including muscles, connective tissues, tendons, ligaments and joints, a therapist can improve a myriad of symptoms to help you to be on your A-game.

But with so many types of massage out there, which are the most beneficial?

THERAPEUTIC MASSAGE

Therapeutic massage - although an umbrella term for various types of massage - will assess each person on a treatment-by-treatment basis. Therapeutic massage tends to encompass a variety of massage methods tailored to you and your symptoms. From tight muscles, headaches, sluggish digestion and stress, these are a handful of issues that can be addressed by therapeutic massage.

However, probably one of the most famous massage treatment is deep tissue. For every keen fitness person, deep tissue massage will have a huge impact on your time exercising. Deep tissue works by - as the name suggests - working on the layers of your muscles. Cross-fibre friction or static pressure using thumbs, fingers or forearms is applied specifically to areas of muscle that are restricted to release the tissue, enabling it to resume its full length and functionality. Usually during a treatment, the therapist will work on a specific part of the body, such as the shoulders, back and neck - a common problem area for many of us.

SPORTS REHAB AND MASSAGE

We've all heard of sports massage and rehab, but when should we 'upgrade' our normal massages to a sports one? Well, the quick answer is for anyone who is active - it's not just for athletes and die-hard fitness addicts. Sports rehab and massage is a fantastic supplement to care for your body pre-and-post activity. We tend to be great at drinking our protein shakes and eating energy balls, but massage is rarely viewed as useful tool to supplement our exercise. Whether recuperating from an injury, preparing the body for a particular sport - such as a marathon or competition - or helping your muscles to be more flexible, sports massage and rehab can help get your body into great shape.

For anyone who has had an injury, from a sprain or strain, all the way through to an operation, you will have scar tissue. Although we may not realise this, scar tissue - whether on the muscles, tendons or ligaments - can cause an array of secondary issues if not treated. And for those looking to get their PB or shave serious minutes off their time, sports rehab will take you to a whole new level by focusing on musculoskeletal health - which muscles are being overused, or which areas are under-performing on a regular basis. The therapist then uses their expertise during treatment so you to get the most out of your body. Sports massage and rehab can help you gain a real competitive edge by increasing the range of motion of various joints and boosting flexibility.

PREGNANCY MASSAGE - ONE FOR THE LADIES!

Getting massages during pregnancy isn't just a blissful, relaxing hour of your day (although that will certainly be one of the benefits) it has a myriad of positive benefits. Many pregnant women view massage as an integral part of their prenatal care. During this time, your body is flooded with hormones, and this can have a massive impact on both mind and body. Studies have shown that massage during your second and third trimester reduces cortisol levels, eases anxiety and morning sickness, plus it has a significant impact in reducing sciatica and girdle pain. The benefits of pregnancy massage cannot be overrated, but it is recommended you liaise with your midwife who can let you know when's best to have a treatment. A trained therapist in pregnancy massage will avoid certain pressure points on the body that can induce an early labour, and will give you peace of mind that you and your bump are in the best of care.

IN CONCLUSION

So, depending on what you want from a massage, there will be one that is best suited to your needs. There isn't a case of one size fits all. Why not try a few different ones, and see which one you prefer? We should try and get into the habit of understanding the importance of massage for a variety of ailments - and focus on the huge benefits it has on our wellbeing. This isn't a luxury, but a necessary tool in preventative healthcare. Massage certainly beats taking prescription drugs and pain killers, which only serve to mask aches and pain. So, whether you have a short or long-term condition, there are a host of massage treatments out there that can be tailored to your needs. Massage has been around for millennia, and there's a good reason why! The amazing health benefits speak for themselves.

UNITASKING: HOW TO MINDFULLY REDUCE STRESS AND ANXIETY BY DANA ZELICHA

The old adage "killing two birds with one stone" has taken on a whole new meaning in the modern working world, where we talk on speaker phone, check our emails, drive to work, and inhale a sandwich all at the same time. Somehow, we manage to get it all done (partially), but did we actually pay attention to what was said on the phone or enjoy the taste of the sandwich? Definitely not.

Multitasking is a common practice with the many distractions people face throughout the day. The belief that multitasking helps us accomplish everything we have to get done, however, is a myth. Research has shown that multitasking negatively affects performance and decreases productivity by up to 40%. Therefore, while many people think that doing multiple things at once is efficient, it is actually counterproductive because the tasks are usually performed with less attention and lower quality.

Instead, the best way to accomplish all of one's tasks is to 'unitask,' or do one thing at a time with full effort and attention. Unitasking involves a conscious commitment to the task at hand and being fully immersed and engaged in the experience. Mindfulness helps to hone unitasking skills because it cultivates a present-moment awareness in which one can carefully focus on what they are currently doing instead of worrying about other obligations or tasks. Unitasking thus produces a higher quality performance and increases productivity by enabling a person to execute a task effectively and efficiently and then move on to the next one.

The focus that mindfulness brings can make a positive difference in both men's and women's lives. But judging by the amount of multitasking women do and the amount of anxiety they feel, women stand to benefit even more. A study by Michigan State University found that women multitask 10 hours more per week than men, and the Anxiety and Depression Association of America reports that women are twice as likely as men to suffer from anxiety in their lifetime. There are also differences between women in the way they handle stress, with single women experiencing less stress and feeling as if they can better manage their stress than their married counterparts.

It may seem like the odds are stacked against women in the stress department, but this does not have to be the case! By recognising sources of stress and becoming mindfully aware of when you start to feel stressed, you can employ effective strategies to help you cope. While it may not be possible to avoid all the stressors of modern life, the first step to finding clarity among the chaos is to stop trying to multitask and to start practicing how to unitask.

HOW CAN I BECOME A UNITASKER?

To unitask, we have to resist the multiple distractions of our environment and our own addictive habits, get very clear about what we want to do, and commit to doing it.

TIPS FOR WORK

Plan your day - 20 minutes at night can save you time at work
How many times have you gone to bed exhausted after a long day, only to find your mind running through every possible scenario of the upcoming day as soon as your head hits the pillow? To calm your mind, get a restful sleep, and avoid feeling overwhelmed the next day, dedicate about 20

minutes BEFORE you go to sleep to write down a plan for the following day. Go through what meetings you have, how much free time you expect to have, and what you can realistically achieve in the designated time slots. Prioritise your tasks and assess if you need to call on any colleagues to help. This will enable you to pre-empt issues that could arise and will leave you feeling prepared for the day - improving your sleep also.

Divide your work day into unitasking episodes and define each one

With the daily plan you make for yourself at night, dedicate a specific time for you to do each task. For example, assign 4:00-5:00 PM for preparing that presentation you haven't had time to work on, and ONLY focus on completing that task with all of your attention and effort. Then, you will be able to complete the task efficiently and be satisfied with the end result, and then tackle the next unitasking episode!

Have a permanent unitasking day

With all the responsibilities you have both at work and at home, it may be challenging to plan out your day to a 'T' and neatly accomplish all of your tasks every day of the week. Ok, it may even feel impossible. Unexpected problems may pop-up throughout the week, but carving out one permanent "Unitasking Day" can help you to feel more in control. Choose one day where you will make it your goal to only focus on one task at a time and to really be attentive to what you are doing. This is a great way to practice Unitasking and help it to become a habit in other days of the week as well, as you will find it adds more order to your day and increases the quality of your work.

Ask yourself "What do I really want (or need) to be doing right now?"

It is easy to feel lost and overwhelmed amid all of your responsibilities, but take time out to assess what you actually need to get done. This will break the mental chatter of all the other different tasks you need to do, help you find clarity, and focus on the most important and urgent task you need to be doing at that moment. Sometimes there is a contradiction between what we want to do and what we need to be doing, and taking a moment to distinguish between the two can help us to mindfully complete what we need to do so that we can then go onto enjoy what we want to do.

EVOLVE WELLNESS CENTRE

10 KENDRICK MEWS, KENSINGTON, SW7 3HG

OPEN

MON.	9:30AM - 9:00PM
TUE-THU.	9:00AM - 9:00PM
FRI.	9:00AM - 8:30PM
SAT.	9:00AM - 6:00PM
SUN.	10:00AM - 6:00PM

 EVOLVEWELLNESSCENTRE.COM

 SOUTH KENSINGTON

Hidden away down a quiet side muse in South Kensington, Evolve Wellness Centre is a sublime spot for all sorts of alternative healing. Whether you're looking to tackle stress, anxiety, back pain, poor focus or posture, you can book treatments such as; Hawaiian Lomilomi massage, posture therapy, Rolfing, spiritual healing and hands on Reiki to put you back in balance. With 2 treatment rooms, 3 studios, and a large workshop room, Evolve Wellness Centre offers a combination of holistic treatments, yoga, Pilates, workshops and occasional community-focused events. With no Wi-Fi, this is a space which ensures your thoughts, your well-being and your intentions are the main focus. Come here if you're looking for a bit of peace and quiet in busy London.

THE FLOATWORKS

UNIT 20D, 17B ST GEORGE WHARF, VAUXHALL, SW8 2LE

OPEN

MON-SUN.	7:30AM - 10:00PM

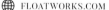 FLOATWORKS.COM

 VAUXHALL

Nowadays, it's hard to find a place where you can simply switch off, but The Floatworks, just a few minutes walk from Vauxhall tube station, thankfully solves this problem. This float centre has 4 pods, each in their own room with a spacious shower to rinse pre and post float. These futuristic looking pods contain 525kg of magnesium rich Epsom salts in water (25cm deep) heated to skin temperature. Climb in, close the lid and allow your body to relax. This is when the sensation of floating begins to take place. Soothing music is played for 10 minutes to help you slow your mind and there is a button to press when you are ready for complete darkness. Free from any sort of distraction, this sensory deprivation takes you into an almost indescribable state of calm. The epitome of mindful meditation, your body has nothing to worry about but your breathe in this cocoon-like device. If you're busy, stressed or feeling burnt out, an hour floating will put you in a place of zen. It's the future of the wellnessphere!

INNER SPACE

36 SHORTS GARDENS, COVENT GARDEN, WC2H 9AB

OPEN

MON-SAT.   10:30AM - 6:00PM
SUN.   CLOSED

🌐 INNERSPACE.ORG.UK

⊖ COVENT GARDEN

Nestled right at the heart of bustling Covent Garden, this meditation and personal development centre is often referred to as, 'London's oasis of calm and insight'. Here, they run courses, seminars and meditations. Courses include creative meditation, practical meditation, relaxation strategies and positive thinking. Most pertinent for busy Londoners, however, are the self-esteem and time management courses. Going against the expensive London grain, Inner Space offers all

activities for free (although they welcome donations), meaning literally anyone can be involved. Enjoy the quiet room - a yellow room lit up in red, where soothing music allows you to relax and let go of everything else.

LIGHT CENTRE BELGRAVIA

7 - 9 ECCLESTON STREET, BELGRAVIA, SW1W 9LX

OPEN

MON-FRI.   7:00AM - 9:30PM
SAT.   8:00AM - 4:00PM
SUN.   CLOSED

🌐 LIGHTCENTREBELGRAVIA.
   CO.UK

⊖ VICTORIA

Found right beside the snazzy Google offices in Victoria, The Light Centre Belgravia is a great place for a digital detox from the outside world. Offering a full range of therapies, as well as yoga, Pilates and mindfulness classes, you're able to book in reflexology, hypnotherapy, ayurvedic practitioners, osteopathy and acupuncture to name just a few. They offer helpful leaflets that explain each therapy and the approach taken by the practitioner. This is helpful if you're not quite sure exactly what you're looking for, or how best to combat certain issues or feelings you might have. The ongoing workshops and courses make this a useful spot not just to master something new, but to develop old practices that need refreshing.

MIND BODY SOUL MINDFUL + WELLNESS SPACES

THE LONDON SLEEP CENTRE

137 HARLEY STREET, MARYLEBONE, W1G 6BF

OPEN

MON-FRI.   9:00AM - 5:00PM

SAT-SUN.   CLOSED

 LONDONSLEEPCENTRE.COM

🚇 REGENT'S PARK

🛜

It's only when you can't sleep that you truly understand how crucial it is to your mood, productivity and processing speed. The London Sleep Centre, a medical clinic on London's renowned Harley Street, diagnose and treat a whole spectrum of troubling sleep disorders. With two consulting rooms and a sleep technician room, they see people with insomnia, night terrors, restless legs syndrome, narcolepsy, chronic fatigue syndrome and sleep apnea, as well as sleep disorders during pregnancy and much more. Taking a holistic approach, their team includes medics, dental sleep experts, psychologists and sleep technologists. Come here and rest assured... you are in good hands.

THE LONDON WELLNESS CENTRE

PORT EAST BUILDING, WEST INDIA QUAY 14 HERTSMERE ROAD, CANARY WHARF, E14 4AF

OPEN

MON-THU.   8:00AM - 7:00PM

FRI.   8:00AM - 4:30PM

SAT.   9:00AM - 2:00PM

SUN.   CLOSED

🌐 THISISLONDONWELLNESS.COM

🚇 CANARY WHARF

The London Wellness Centre offers a full range of treatments to prevent and cure both physical and mental issues. Though the clinic itself is simple and unassuming, care and attention is given to each individual, with extensive assessments and consultations before each treatment. Offering chiropractic treatment, psychotherapy, hypnotherapy, massage, sports physio, gynaecology, chiropody and podiatry, they bring together the many different components that make up your overall wellbeing. Their friendly staff and strong belief that 'prevention is always better than a cure' means they do their best to help people realise and reduce any underlying health issues before they become a real and firmly rooted problem. Conveniently close to the big city firms, The London Wellness Centre is one for the little black book if you're sat at a desk throughout the day – they'll help you to move, eat and think better than before.

THE MINDFULNESS PROJECT

6 FITZROY SQUARE, FITZROVIA, W1T 5DX

OPEN

SEE WEBSITE FOR TIMETABLE

 LONDONMINDFUL.COM

 WARREN STREET /
GREAT PORTLAND STREET

Situated on the second floor of the Georgian house owned by the Georgian Society, The Mindfulness Project is - as its name suggests - completely dedicated to mindfulness. All practise here is completely evidence-based, led by a strong team of advisors, support staff and mindfulness teachers, with the aim of providing an innovative platform for sharing mindfulness with as many people as possible. The Mindfulness Project runs a myriad of retreats and classes, from mindfulness for work, to self-compassion and mindfulness for anxiety and depression. Most

popular is the 8-week mindfulness course, which includes a full one-day intensive retreat. Founded by Alexandra Frey and Autumn Totton in 2013, this is a space in which you can learn hacks to be kinder to yourself, from big to small, formal and informal.

NEAL'S YARD REMEDIES

2 NEAL'S YARD, COVENT GARDEN, WC2H 9DP

OPEN

MON-SAT.   10:00AM - 8:00PM
SUN.   11:00AM - 6:30PM

 NEALSYARDREMEDIES.COM

 COVENT GARDEN

Neal's Yard Remedies, London's well established organic apothecary, recently opened their newly renovated therapy rooms in Covent Garden. The venue is located directly across from their flagship store in Neal's Yard - the signature dark blue tiles around the entrance make it easy to spot in the colourful courtyard. The therapy rooms offer holistic and specialised treatments including aromatherapy, acupuncture, and counselling, in addition to a variety of massage styles. Bespoke herbal medicines are available for those seeking natural remedies to their

ailments. There's something for everyone at the Neal's Yard Remedies therapy rooms, pop by for a treatment that is good for you and the environment.

THE BREATHING TREE

BY **REBECCA DENNIS,** THE BREATHING TREE

The very first thing we do when we make our entrance into the world is breathe, and it is the last thing we do when we exit. With that in mind we may as well have a good relationship with our breath. The most important thing in life is to breathe - after all, we live to breathe and we breathe to live. We cannot exist without it.

We teach our young to walk, communicate, bathe, eat and socialise, yet educating them about the healing power of their breath is not a priority. I want to encourage people to be aware of their breath and share the multitude of wonderful benefits that emerge from breathing consciously. How we breathe is indicative of how we can feel more connected and feel about life. The way we feel directly affects the way we think and the way we think affects how we feel. Our breath correlates with every feeling, thought, experience and emotion.

A little statistic for you: we inhale and exhale around 20,000 times a day, yet most of us pay little attention to how we breathe or how deeply it affects us. In our increasingly demanding and complex world very few people are aware of the detrimental effects that improper breathing can have on our health and general well-being. In modern day life we are tied to our phones, our laptops, our iPads. In a world where we are more connected than ever with people through the internet and social media people feel more alone and disconnected.

Sometimes we literally forget to take a breath. 'I'm so stressed out, I can't breathe' and 'I just need some space to breathe'. This is where conscious breathing comes in as an effective method of reducing stress and pain.

The pattern goes a bit like this: to balance work commitments, lifestyle and family life. There is a lot of pressure in today's society for everyone to perform, and there seems to be just one pace of life - fast. We are multitasking, hitting deadlines, and situations put us under pressure. As a result, we are burning more energy than we need to, just taking care of business. Stimulation, activity and demands are all around us. Often, we are on high-speed-runaway-train mode and our responsibilities, commitments and worries prevent us from feeling calm and staying in the moment.

We all have our own unique breathing pattern, a bit like our thumb print. Our breath patterns show where we are at in the world, and as a breath coach, I am trained to read the patterns. When you observe a baby lying in a cot you will notice their breath is in their belly, midsection and chest and there are no blockages or restrictions. The same is with toddlers however the majority of teenagers and adults are either chest breathers, belly breathers or breath holders. Transformational Breath helps us to understand and clear these restricted breathing patterns.

The majority of us are only using a third of our respiratory capacity and by practicing this technique we open up our respiratory system and release emotional and physical tension and blockages. This helps our overall wellbeing on a physical, mental and emotional level. Breathwork is much like therapy but without having to do the talking. It's not about going over and over the story but letting it go. Our body is a biological recording of our past and when we experience emotions such as fear or anger for example our physiology goes into chaos. Our heart rate increases, our digestion and immune system may be affected. We activate our sympathetic nervous system, our flight or fight mechanism and release adrenalin and cortisol. Our body remembers everything and our breath is always listening.

Is it any wonder that there is an alarming rise

in mental illness and people being medicated for anxiety, panic attacks and depression. Transformational Breath is like taking the breath to the gym or for an MOT. We are resetting and recalibrating the systems of our body with the breath.

Just as we blink our eyes, our heart beats and digestive system works we breathe automatically but with the breath when we become aware of our breath we can also control and be conscious about how we breathe.

The breath is the bridge linking our mind and body. The practice of deep breathing techniques helps to stimulate our parasympathetic nervous system, bringing us to a calm state. Diaphragmatic breathing stimulates the Parasympathetic Nervous System (PNS) which allows the body to rest and digest, slowing the heart rate, lowering blood pressure and respiratory rate and diverting blood supply towards the digestive and reproductive systems.

When the Parasympthetic Nervous System is active, the Sympathetic Nervous System (SNS) becomes less active - they counteract each other. The SNS raises heart rate, blood pressure and respiratory rate, diverting blood to the brain and skeletal muscle in readiness for fight or flight.

By deactivating or overriding the SNS, we can interrupt the vicious cycle of adrenaline and cortisol which contribute to chronic stress levels and predispose us to panic attacks and anxiety.

Our breath is our anchor and even better it's free. We cannot necessarily control what is going on around us but we can take care of how it affects us on the inside. By being present and practicing these breathing techniques every day we can feel lighter, freer, more focussed and relaxed.

CONSCIOUS CONNECTED BREATH EXERCISE

Here's a simple exercise to practice just 1 - 2 minutes every day. If you miss a day don't worry as we don't want to make it another chore. Transformational Breath is a cutting-edge breath technique to empower and help you to be the best version of you.

+ **Prop yourself up on the bed at a semi-reclined angle with cushions or pillows behind you so your chest is higher than your legs.**

+ **Make sure you are warm and comfortable, and that your head and neck are supported.**

+ **Place your hands on your lower abdomen - a few inches below the navel. Relax the jaw and open the mouth wide and take a deep inhalation, belly should rise like a balloon, and exhale with a quick, gentle sigh.**

+ **Stay present with the inhale and the exhale. Inhalation should be about twice as long as the exhalation. Exhalation should be quiet and relaxed like a soft sigh.**

+ **Keep the breath connected so no pauses between breaths and coming in and out like a wave motion. Repeat up to 1-2 minutes and notice any physical sensations in the body.**

+ **Rest for one minute as you return to a normal breathing pattern - breathing through the nose.**

SLEEP WELL, LIVE BETTER

BY **DR NEIL STANLEY**

"…for Sleepe is that golden chaine that ties health and our bodies together".

Thomas Dekker, English dramatist (1609)

Everyone knows New York as 'the city that never sleeps' but this saying has become equally true of London. In many ways, this is an attractive aspect of living in such a large and fast-paced city, but it does mean that getting a good night's sleep is that much harder. For those that feel they can function fine on late nights and early starts, the usual response is to ask, 'why should that matter?' On the one hand, people are becoming more actively engaged in attending to their nutrition and exercise to promote good health, but on the other, they are failing to recognise the importance that good sleep plays in your personal wellbeing. Much like food, water and air, sleep is a biological necessity.

Scientific studies show that the long-term risks of poor sleep lead to an increased likelihood of developing conditions such as cardiovascular disease, Alzheimer's, depression, emotional disorders, obesity and diabetes. Fundamentally, sleep affects the brain and the nervous system. For reasons such as this, sleep needs to be taken more seriously.

For those people that don't have a medical sleep disorder, but struggle to get a good night's sleep, stress is the number one cause of short term sleeping difficulties. The issues that people let bubble under the surface commonly result in sleepless nights, which in itself, becomes a vicious and self-perpetuating circle – the less you sleep, the worse you feel, the worse you feel, the harder it becomes to sleep. Factors such as volitional sleep deprivation (work, lifestyle, shift work), poor sleep habits and environmental disruptions (noise, light, movements) also play a large part in this particular problem.

HOW DOES SLEEP HELP TO ENSURE YOUR WELLBEING?

Firstly, poor sleep is known to compromise your immune system, so sleeping better will reduce your chances of getting an infection and ensure a faster recovery from any sort of illness.

Secondly, getting enough sleep is vital for our physical, mental and emotional health, which is important to remember because when it comes to feeling and looking good, diet and exercise are prioritised and the importance of sleep is regularly overlooked.

Studies have proved that poor sleep leads to an increase in appetite, fat production and weight gain. This is not just a consequence of long-term sleep deprivation, increase in hunger and appetite occur after just one night of reduced sleep. Studies have shown a link between length of sleep and body mass index (BMI). Those who sleep for less than seven hours a night are likely to have a higher BMI than those who regularly have a good night's sleep. The disruption of our 'hunger hormones' also makes us more likely to eat irregularly, snack between meals, season our food excessively and eat fewer vegetables - none of which contribute to a well-balanced diet.

The amount of sleep we get is linked to how active we are and how energetic we feel. Studies show that people who have trouble sleeping at night or feel excessively sleepy during the day have less energy and are less active; often this leads to irritability, moodiness and disinhibition. If you've had a good night's sleep, you're more likely to spring out of bed in the mood for physical activity or exercise. When you don't get enough sleep, these everyday activities become arduous and you are putting yourself at a significantly higher risk of sustaining a sports related injury.

HOW CAN WE IMPROVE OUR SLEEP?

First and foremost, your bedroom should be your sanctuary. There should be nothing in your bedroom that is not there for sleep - no computer, no phones, no television or tablet. Your bedroom is intended for your bed, not for work, games, pets or films.

Your bedroom needs to be dark, if you can stand at one side and see the opposite wall then your room is too light. It needs to be quiet. If you don't look out onto a busy road, then keep the window slightly open to allow fresh air to circulate the room. Ideally, it should be neither too hot nor too cold and perhaps most importantly, you need the biggest, most comfortable bed you can afford. In a city with such a vibrant night life, ensuring a dark and quiet bedroom can be difficult but blackout blinds or heavy curtains can help reduce light. Noise is generally trickier to deal with so if it's a problem, consider using earplugs specifically designed for bedtime.

You need to have a relaxed body to get good sleep and this means having a clear mind. How do you quieten you mind? Well that is down to you. Some people find reading helps, or camomile tea, mindfulness or yoga. Different things work for different people but there are a whole host of calming exercises and techniques out there to help you unwind.

With today's busy lifestyles, getting enough sleep can be difficult. We need to re-evaluate how we view sleep. Determine how many hours a night you need to sleep and then set aside time for it. Getting enough sleep is a decision. We need to see sleep as a vital link in the 'well-being triangle' - alongside a healthy diet and plenty of exercise.

Sleep well, eat better and move more.

DISCONNECT TO RECONNECT

IN CONVERSATION WITH JODY SHIELD BY **THE LONDON WELLNESS GUIDE**

Jody Shield is an inspirational speaker, author, meditation teacher and intuitive healer. She is also the first European meditation ambassador for global brand Lululemon Athletica.

Now, more than ever, we are connected. Connected to our smartphones and computer screens, connected to our emails and WhatsApp groups, connected in a way that we have never been before. Part of a social media culture, we are constantly stimulated and easily distracted from the present moment. The line between work and life has become blurred because it's increasingly difficult to log off.

Having spent long hours and late nights working in the corporate world of advertising, Jody speaks passionately about the growing need to remedy the effects of burnout. Her own career change was inspired by the desire to help those that struggle with managing intense workloads and the pressure they put upon themselves. "Living in a fast moving, fast-paced society" says Jody, "it's easy to get addicted to working very hard, the non-stop energy of this city supports that." The downside of this is that people are giving themselves no time to unwind. Jody always advises people to listen to their body, "if you are consistently drained, exhausted and running on empty, if you are unhappy and unbalanced, then this is not healthy. We are not robots. We have not been designed to work 12 hours straight, we are designed to rest and to find pockets of the day to recharge."

A believer in the power of holistic healing and successfully running her own self-help workshops and private sessions, Jody tells her clients, "It's always about how we can raise our energy levels, how we can feel higher, we are looking for those moments that release endorphins and give us this natural high." One way of doing this is by making what Jody calls 'a gratitude list'. "Have a list of things you really want to attract into your life, by writing them out it will help you realise your own goals and what's important to you. When you write out what you are grateful for,

include how it makes you feel, close your eyes and take a minute to dwell on those happy feelings. This helps to pump endorphins around your body that make you feel good."

According to Jody, the key is to build positive habits into your morning routine – why not start the day off with a guided meditation? While it can be hard to find time for yourself, it's that much easier once you've learnt how to calm and focus your thoughts. "The trick is the feeling" advises Jody, "if you can notice a difference in how you feel then you will keep doing these things."

For many people, it's not easy to stay positive. "We collect the moments where we felt rejected, upset, abandoned and uncertain, and these emotions become our baggage" insists Jody, "burnout in the workplace very often comes as a result of failing to address the baggage we carry and this is made easier to avoid when we are constantly in a state of distraction." Addiction of any sort, which includes workaholism, is a form of escape and a means of resistance. The fine line between control and loss of control is something that Jody helps people confront and come to terms with. "People are scared of losing it and letting their baggage fall out on the floor. Tubes are late and people let us down, there is nothing we can do about it. This loss of control is something we're all afraid of to varying degrees, but it's how you cope with it that makes you or breaks you."

Jody advocates specific techniques that can be used anywhere at anytime to bring you back to the present moment. Tapping is her favourite tool to breakthrough resistance and channel the mind. A simple variation of this is to bunch one hand into a fist and start tapping the V of your collarbone as if you're gently knocking on a door. Not only will this snap you out of your daydreams but it is a very calming method that is said to evoke the feeling of being winded as a baby.

The technique of tapping can also be used in a more subtle way with one of Jody's fingertip tapping exercises. To do this, start tapping your little fingertip on your thumb and say "peace", then move on to your ring finger and thumb and say "begins" then the middle finger and thumb and say "with" and the index finger say "me". Get into a rhythm and once you feel calmer simply switch the first word for another positive word such as: hope, strength, change, focus, love, or courage. If you're feeling stressed or anxious outside a meeting, or before a presentation, then take 5 minutes and just go through this out loud or in your head.

Another tool for people struggling in a battle with their mind is simply to say, "I surrender" and repeat it to themselves a few times. A strong word which Jody says, "gives a signal to your brain to just stop and let go." If you feel anxious feelings coming on just say "come out" because fear and anxiety are more powerful when they are hidden away. "Party with your anxiety" urges Jody, "See it, invite it in, acknowledge it and then let it go".

Knowing when to hold on and when to let go is an important skill. Life is a journey, and inevitably we pick up varying amounts of emotional baggage along the way, but knowing what we need, what we don't, and how best to manage it, will help you to navigate the terrain a great deal better.

WELLNESS GLOSSARY

ACUPRESSURE A traditional form of Chinese massage where pressure is applied to specific points on the body to stimulate energy flow (Qi), ease muscle tension and promote relaxation.

ACUPUNCTURE Traditional Chinese healing technique where very fine needles are inserted into energy centres (called meridians) in order to restore energy balance and activate the body's healing response.

ALEXANDER TECHNIQUE A technique used to re-educate the body by building greater awareness of posture and movement. It is thought to reduce instances of muscle and joint strain, minimise pain and improve posture.

AEROBIC/ANAEROBIC EXERCISE Aerobic means 'with oxygen' and includes exercises such as walking, jogging and cycling. Anaerobic means 'without oxygen' and involves short bursts of strenuous muscular exercise.

ANTIOXIDANT Antioxidants, such as Vitamins A, C and E, reduce the oxidation speed of other molecules in the body, therefore slowing the production of free radicals and reducing cell damage.

AROMATHERAPY The use of plant oils within therapeutic treatments, such as massages and body wraps. Different oils are believed to have unique healing properties and are used to soothe body and mind.

ASANAS In yoga, asanas are the various physical shapes and postures that make up a practice. Most branches of yoga involve a routine of asanas to help promote awareness in body and mind.

AYURVEDIC MEDICINE Originating in ancient India, this system of healing incorporates nutrition, herbal medicine, aromatherapy, massage and meditation. 'Ayurvedic' can be translated to mean 'life knowledge'.

BODYWORK Relating to a wide variety of hands-on therapies, including massage, manipulation therapy and energy healing. Techniques aim to improve posture, movement and self-awareness.

BODY WRAP Spa treatment where strips of cloth are soaked in a heated herbal solution and wrapped around the body to promote relaxation, draw out impurities and assist in detoxification. Varieties include the 'Seaweed Wrap' - popular for its nutrient-rich properties.

BOTANICALS The use of natural plant parts and extracts for their therapeutic properties or medicinal effects. Botanicals are commonly found in herbal medicine and cosmetic products.

BMI BMI is calculated by dividing weight in kilograms by height in metres to find out whether an adult's weight is healthy. An ideal BMI for a healthy adult is between 18.5 and 24.9.

COMPLEMENTARY AND ALTERNATIVE MEDICINE (CAM) Complementary medicines can be used alongside conventional therapies; alternative medicines aim to replace conventional therapies. Both are thought to assist the healing process.

CHINESE MEDICINE A traditional Chinese healthcare system used across China for thousands of years. Techniques include massage, herbal remedies, acupuncture and Qi Gong (energy balancing).

'CLEAN EATING' A contemporary term used to describe a way of eating that focuses on eating whole, unprocessed foods in their most natural form, avoiding convenience foods and additives.

COLONIC IRRIGATION A therapeutic technique that involves flushing out the colon with filtered water in order to remove trapped impurities and prevent toxins from recycling in the bloodstream.

COLOUR THERAPY (CHROMOTHERAPY) Dating back to ancient Egypt, Colour Therapy is based on the concept that colour has vibrational energy that can heal the body. Lights, crystals and fabrics may be used for their therapeutic properties.

DEEP-TISSUE MASSAGE The application of slow,

intense pressure to help align deep layers of muscle and connective tissue in order to improve agility and posture, and relieve stress and pain.

DETOX A 'detox' is intended to cleanse the body and rid it of built-up poisons and toxins. Detoxing may involve abstaining from certain foods, drinks or chemical substances.

DNA ANALYSIS Various procedures that allow an individual's DNA to be analysed with the intention of recommending a particular way of living and eating to suit their unique genetic make up.

DOSHA An ancient Ayurvedic term used to describe three mind-body qualities that all people are believed to possess (Vata, Pitta and Kapha). Ayurvedic practise aims to balance these qualities within people.

ENDORPHINS Natural chemical messengers in the body that are released during exercise, sex, laughter and when physically hurt. This process helps relieve pain and promotes feelings of wellbeing.

ESSENTIAL OILS Aromatic oils are extracted from flowers, fruits, herbs, roots and trees. They maintain an essence of the plant, either in smell or taste, and are thought to have therapeutic benefits.

EXFOLIATION Use of a natural bristle brush or exfoliating scrub to remove old, dead skin and impurities, and stimulate the circulatory system. Commonly used before a range of spa treatments.

FENG SHUI A Chinese tradition where furniture and objects are arranged to optimise a harmonious flow of energy between all things. This is believed to enhance health, happiness, wealth and relationships.

FLOATATION THERAPY Use of an enclosed tank filled with warm water and Epsom salts to create a dark, peaceful environment. Thought to be similar to conditions in the womb, and therefore promote deep relaxation.

GLYCAEMIC INDEX (GI) GI measures the effect of certain foods on blood sugar levels. Foods that have a low GI will impact less on blood sugar levels (and are therefore healthier) than those with a high GI.

GREEN TEA Tea that is made from unfermented tea leaves, usually sourced from Japan or China. Green tea is packed with nutrients and antioxidants, and thought to be highly beneficial to health.

HIGH-INTENSITY INTERVAL TRAINING (HIIT) A cardiovascular workout that alternates short bursts of anaerobic exercise with low intensity recovery periods. A popular way to boost metabolic rate, and increase strength and endurance.

HOLISTIC MEDICINE A system of healthcare that considers each person as a whole, taking into account psychological, physical, social and spiritual influences throughout the process of diagnosis and treatment.

HOMEOPATHY Based on the principle that 'like cures like', each remedy contains miniscule quantities of substances that would (in larger doses) cause the symptoms they aim to treat. Thought to trigger the body's healing response.

HYDROTHERAPY Includes a range of water-based therapies thought to relieve pain and enhance wellbeing. Exercises are often used to alleviate symptoms of arthritis and other rheumatic complaints.

INDOOR CYCLING A form of exercise that focuses on high-intensity workouts that build strength and endurance. Classes take place in a group setting using stationary bikes.

INFRARED TREATMENT Lamps and infrared saunas expose the body to far-infrared light, which mimics sunlight but without the harmful UV rays. Said to relieve sore muscles and joints, and even help detoxify.

IRIDOLOGY Based on the principle that patterns, characteristics and colours in the iris (the coloured part of the eye) can be examined to assess health and even diagnose disease.

KINESIOLOGY/APPLIED KINESIOLOGY The science of human movement and how it relates to health. Applied Kinesiology is a system that aims to diagnose and treat disease by assessing and improving muscle strength.

MATCHA LATTE Made using stoneground green tea leaves mixed with hot milk or a milk alternative. Provides the same nutritional benefits and antioxidants as if one were eating the whole tea leaf.

MEDITATION Originating from ancient India, meditation is an exercise in training the mind to achieve a greater sense of awareness (mindfulness). Thought to promote relaxation and wellbeing.

METABOLIC RATE The speed at which the body burns fuel and uses it for energy. Metabolic rate can vary due to age, sex, genetic traits, physical activity and the proportion of muscle to fat in the body.

MICROBIOME The human microbiome is the community of microbes and microorganisms that call the body home. The human body relies on this 'mini-ecosystem' for a range of vital functions.

MICRONUTRIENTS Substances or chemical elements that are needed by the body in very small quantities - for example, Vitamin C and Calcium. Micronutrients ensure proper health and development throughout life.

MINDFULNESS The practice of focusing on 'the present moment' without being distracted by, or judging, thoughts, feelings or sensations. Used as a therapeutic technique to enhance wellbeing.

MYLK A medieval spelling of the word 'milk' used to describe the range of dairy-free milk alternatives, including coconut, almond and oat milk. Suitable for Vegan and dairy-free diets.

NATUROPATHY A collection of natural therapies that aim to treat the causes, rather than symptoms, of disease. Treatments focus on nutrition, herbal medicine, homeopathy and mind-body therapies.

OMEGA-3 A class of essential fatty acid that is commonly found in fish, particularly salmon and other 'oily' varieties. Thought to help lower levels of bad cholesterol and prevent heart disease.

OMEGA-6 An essential fatty acid that is sourced from food, such as nuts, seeds and plant oils. It is important to get the right balance between Omegas 3 and 6 as too much Omega 6 can cause severe damage.

ORGANIC Organic foods are produced without the use of chemicals, such as growth hormones, pesticides and fertilizers. Promotes a more natural way of growing and rearing food.

PILATES A system of low-impact, body conditioning exercises that combine apparatus and mat-work to develop flexibility, physical strength, posture and enhance mental awareness.

PLACEBO A substance that has no medicinal effect, but can nonetheless create health improvements known as 'the placebo effect' - based on the physiological effect of taking a 'remedy'.

POWER YOGA A more energetic form of yoga involving a sequence of postures (asanas) that flow together, building heat in the body. Improves strength and flexibility, and promotes greater awareness.

PREVENTIVE MEDICINE A holistic approach to health that uses conventional and alternative methods to prevent or reverse disease, rather than focus on curing existing ill health (as in conventional medicine).

'PROATS' A combination of the words 'protein' and 'oats'. A term used for an oatmeal-based meal (usually breakfast) with additional protein, for example protein powder or quark.

PROBIOTICS Probiotic foods contain good bacteria that help maintain a healthy gut. Sources include fermented foods like natural yoghurt, quark, kefir, live sauerkraut, miso and kimchi.

PREBIOTICS Prebiotic foods feed the good bacteria in the gut and therefore help maintain optimum health. Sources include oats, fennel, apples, garlic, leeks, cold potatoes and onions.

SHIATSU A Japanese massage technique that focuses on specific pressure points on the body, known as meridian points. These are thought to stimulate the body's healing response and free blocked energy.

STRESS MANAGEMENT A range of techniques that are designed to improve the day-to-day function of an individual by minimising the effects of stress. Usually includes exercise, relaxation and visualisation.

SUPERFOODS Nutrient-rich foods, often high in compounds such as antioxidants, fibre or fatty acids, which are thought to be beneficial to physical and mental health and help prevent disease.

TAI CHI A Chinese martial art, often described as 'meditation in motion', thought to reduce stress and improve agility. Practitioners will move through a series of postures, coordinated by the breath.

THERAPEUTIC MASSAGE The therapeutic manipulation of soft body tissues - an effective way to decrease muscle pain, reduce spasms and improve movement, while also promoting deep relaxation.

TUI NA Central to Traditional Chinese Medicine, Tui Na is a massage therapy thought to balance the flow of energy in the body and release toxins through a range of acupressure techniques.

TURMERIC LATTE A health-promoting latte alternative, the Turmeric Latte is a mixture of cold-pressed turmeric juice and nut milk. It is high in antioxidants and thought to have anti-inflammatory properties.

VEGAN A diet and/or lifestyle that is free from meat, fish, poultry and animal by-products. Veganism avoids the cruelty and exploitation of animals for food, clothing or any other purpose.

VEGETARIAN A diet and/or lifestyle that doesn't contain meat products. There are various types of vegetarianism, including ovo-vegetarian (dairy-free) and lacto-vegetarian (egg-free).

VINOTHERAPY A therapeutic skin treatment that uses antioxidant-rich grape residue (leftover from winemaking) within scrubs and masks to exfoliate the skin and reduce signs of ageing.

WATSU A healing treatment that combines Shiatsu massage and water therapy, involving pressure-point massage and stretches. It is performed in a warm pool and is thought to relieve stress and muscle tension.

WEIGHT TRAINING The use of free weights and weight machines to perform strength-building exercises that are designed to develop and tone lean muscle mass, while also raising the metabolic rate.

WELLNESS A state of good health, often related to the active pursuit of a more positive quality of life. Wellness encompasses physical, mental, spiritual and emotional health and wellbeing.

YOGA Ancient Hindu discipline, popular for its ability to enhance physical and mental wellbeing. Yoga involves a series of postures (asanas) and breathing exercises, mindfully performed, to improve bodily awareness.

ZEN The Buddhist idea that enlightenment can be reached through meditation, contemplation and intuition rather than faith. Often used to describe a state of focus where body and mind are in harmony.

A-Z LIST OF VENUES